William Heirens:

The True Story of the Lipstick Killer

by
Jack Rosewood
&
Dwayne Walker

**Historical Serial Killers and Murderers
True Crime by Evil Killers
Volume 13**

Copyright © 2015 by Wiq Media

ALL RIGHTS RESERVED

No part of this book may be reproduced, stored in a retrieval system, or transmitted in any form or by any means, electronic, mechanical, photocopying, recording, scanning, or otherwise, without the prior written permission of the publisher.

ISBN-13:978-1530019465

DISCLAIMER

This serial killer biography includes quotes from those closely involved in the case of American serial killer William George Heirens, and it is not the author's intention to defame or intentionally hurt anyone involved. The interpretation of the events leading up to Heirens' arrest and capture and subsequent execution are the author's as a result of researching the true crime murder. Any comments made about the psychopathic or sociopathic behavior of Heirens are the sole opinion and responsibility of the person quoted.

Go to <u>www.jackrosewood.com</u>

and get this E-Book for free!

Contents

INTRODUCTION 1

CHAPTER 1: A Seemingly Normal Family 4

   Repressed Sexuality: The First Signs of the Lipstick Killer? 6

CHAPTER 2: Early Criminal Activity 12

   Walking through Darkness 14

   Heirens' First Arrest 15

   Reformatory Days 17

A Most Precocious Sociopath 21

CHAPTER 3: The Murder Spree 23

   The Murder of Josephine Ross 24

   The Frances Brown Murder 26

   The Kidnapping, Murder, and Dismemberment of Suzanne Degnan 28

   Reasons for Murder? 31

   Other Suspects 32

CHAPTER 4: The Nightmare Ends 37

   The Arrest 37

   William Heirens in Custody 40

The Polygraph Examination 41

The Press Gets Involved 42

CHAPTER 5: Awaiting Trial 44

Dr. Jekyll and Mr. Hyde 45

Insanity or Hoax? 46

Mom and Dad 52

Other Evidence 56

A Plea Bargain? 60

Heirens Saves His Life 63

CHAPTER 6: Life in Prison 68

At Home with His Peers 69

Efforts to Be Released 73

Questioning the Evidence 75

Richard Russell Thomas 83

CHAPTER 7: The Final Years of the Lipstick Killer 85

Attempts at Parole and Other Legal Maneuvers 85

The Death of the Lipstick Killer 89

Conclusion 91

The making of a serial killer 95

It leaves us always asking why 97

Serial killers think they're unique – but they're not 100

Nature vs. nurture? 101

Going inside the mind: Psychopathy and other mental illnesses 103

Top signs of a serial killer 111

Trademarks of a serial killer 114

More books by Jack Rosewood 120

Here's Your Free Gift 130

A Note From The Author 131

Introduction

"Heavens sake catch me before I kill more I cannot control myself" was found scrawled in lipstick on the wall of a Chicago apartment on December 11, 1945. Under the bizarre inscription lay the mutilated body of Frances Brown, who was the second victim of serial killer William Heirens, the man who would later achieve national infamy for his short but brutal reign of terror on the city of Chicago. Once Heirens was identified as the killer, he was quickly given the moniker "the Lipstick Killer" for the unholy epitaph he left in Brown's apartment.

An examination of Heirens' life reveals that despite a solid home and academic potential, sometimes even the most seemingly stable person sometimes walks a fine line between upright citizen and serial killer.

William Heirens possessed all the attributes of a standard serial killer: a lack of empathy for other humans, an overinflated ego and sense of self, and a deviant sexuality; but Heirens' background was different than most of his fellow murderers.

By the standards of 1930s and '40s America, Heirens grew up in a strict but stable home where he was afforded plenty of opportunities. His parents remained married until his murder spree and there is no evidence that his father abused his mother, Heirens or his younger brother. There is also no evidence that Heirens was ever abused physically or sexually by any other family members, teachers, or strangers.

Likewise, there is also no evidence that a young William Heirens ever abused his younger brother or any of the other younger children in his neighborhood. Also, unlike other notorious serial killers, Heirens was never known to have tortured or mutilated animals.

Despite the apparent normal childhood, something disturbing was lurking beneath the façade. There was something evil within William Heirens that was fighting to get out.

Eventually the evil within William Heirens was released on at least three victims in Chicago, which left that city in fear until he was apprehended. But Heirens' killing spree and subsequent arrest and conviction are only part of the Lipstick Killer's story.

The Lipstick Killer committed his crimes decades before the term "serial killer" was first coined and even longer before DNA testing was a tool in the arsenal of police departments. His arrest and conviction was obtained by hardnosed, old school police officers of a bygone era who used tactics that would today at best get the arrest thrown out of court and at worst end up with the arrest of the police.

Heirens' evolution from apparently normal all-American kid, to juvenile delinquent, and eventually serial killer also gives some important insight into the genesis of a serial killer.

The debate over whether a person is born or made a serial killer may never be resolved, but the case of the Lipstick Killer reveals all killers – no matter their backgrounds – exhibit signs in their childhoods that point towards their future endeavors. William Heirens is the perfect example that not every serial killer abused animals or other children when he or she was young, but every serial exhibits signs that family members, teachers, and authorities should not fail to recognize.

CHAPTER 1:
A Seemingly Normal Family

William Heirens' life began rather inauspiciously on November 15, 1928 in Evanston, Illinois. Heirens' family was of Luxemburg-German descent and no relative from either side of the family tree were known to suffer from alcoholism, insanity, or abuse of any type. If one were to view the Heirens family during the 1930s, it would appear as the quintessential middle-American, Rockwellesque family. By all accounts, Mr. and Mrs. Heirens took their marriage vows seriously and they both worked long hours to provide for William and his younger brother.

Despite being a Roman Catholic family, the Heirens instilled a strong Protestant work ethic in William and his younger brother by always being gainfully employed. Mr. Heirens owned a flower shop for a while, but after the Great Depression hit he was forced to sell the shop and look for employment elsewhere. Eventually, he found a position at Carnegie Steel where he worked for several years as an investigator.

Mr. Heirens position as an investigator was a reflection of one of the primary values in which he believed and imparted on his two sons – law and order. William was brought up with clear ethics and morals concerning right and wrong and a respect for the law. After Heirens was arrested for his murder spree, he indicated to psychiatrists who examined him that he knew what he did was wrong, but he never qualified if he thought it was morally or legally so.

In the end, the belief in law and order that the Heirens family imbued in their two sons was not enough to keep William from committing countless burglaries and three murders.

William and his brother were expected to help with both parents in chores around the house and William was usually employed part-time, when he was not incarcerated in juvenile facilities, throughout his childhood. Mr. Heirens was able to obtain part-time employment for William during the summer months before he went off to college.

Mrs. Heirens was equally ambitious and hardworking as she worked part-time as a baker while raising William and his younger brother. Even with the Great Depression raging, breaking up families throughout the United States, the Heirens family was always able to provide William and his brother with food and a stable household.

William Heirens may not have been raised in a wealthy household, but few kids were in the Depression era 1930s, although he apparently was never in need of food, shelter, or ethical instruction.

Although not all serial killers were physically and/or sexually abused as children, even many of the ones who were not, such as Jeffrey Dahmer, felt the effects of an unstable home, usually through divorce. Heirens' situation then, although not totally unique, was definitely an outlier among serial killers.

Besides the familial stability that William Heirens experienced as a child, his parents believed that William and his brother needed a solid religious foundation in their lives.

Repressed Sexuality: The First Signs of the Lipstick Killer?

For most people, religion provides structure and a purpose to life that is usually positive. Religion gives can give a person a code to live by and a way to connect with the wider world and develop empathy for other living creatures.

Besides providing a sound moral and ethical foundation, religion is often the first place where many people are introduced to literacy as they learn how to read the sacred texts of their particular religion. Religion also provides many people with a positive sense of identity and belonging to a particular group that is both comforting and protective.

In Heirens' case, religious education may have partially had the opposite effect.

As stated above, the Heirens household was Roman Catholic and by all accounts the family followed the doctrines of the Church closely. In particular, discussions about sexuality were taboo in the Heirens house and considered "dirty."

Heirens claimed that when he was eleven years old he witnessed a couple having sex, which he then reported to his mother who responded that sex was bad and leads to disease and that he should forget about what he saw. Heirens claimed that he followed his mother's advice and tried to forget what he saw and even tried to repress most of his sexual feelings.

But eventually Heirens' sexual feelings would be manifested in the most unhealthy and bizarre ways.

According to Heirens' parents, he never showed any signs of sexual curiosity, but in a family that viewed sex as a dirty act, it is no wonder that young Heirens hid most of his fantasies from his parents. After Heirens was arrested for murder, he was submitted to lengthy interviews and examinations by leading psychiatrists from the Chicago area. A number of the interviews centered on Heirens' sexuality, which was considered far from normative.

In the interviews, it was revealed that he was still a virgin and he claims that he never masturbated until his murder spree. To Heirens, pre-marital sex was one of the worst sins a person could commit and masturbation was essentially pre-marital sex.

Over the course of the interviews, Heirens claimed that he developed a sexual fetish for women's underwear at age nine. Heirens' underwear fetish is important and played a central role in his murder spree as he professed that his criminal career began by stealing women's underwear from laundry rooms in apartment basements and open houses.

Many normal, healthy people have fetishes, but Heirens' underwear fetish developed into a bizarre obsession.

Heirens told the psychiatrists that he never had sexual dreams of women, but that instead he "dreamed of women's underwear." In fact, the Lipstick Killer's dreams of women's underwear became quite detailed as he told the doctors: "They were laid out nicely in drawers. In my last wet dream there was a picture of going through windows. It was usually along that line."

William Heirens' repressed sexuality and abnormal sexual behaviors and fetishes seem to have formed the core of his disturbed personality, but there were a number of other factors that seem to have contributed to his personality disorder.

More Cracks in the Façade

After William Heirens was born, he was raised in the middle class suburb of Lincolnwood, Illinois. Reports indicate that the young Heirens had few friends and was for the most part a loner growing up, although there is no evidence that he was the victim of bullying any more than normal for a child.

As already intimated above concerning sexuality, William Heirens was also not very close to his parents and never talked with them about certain issues, but those relationships should be considered in the context of the period. Today, modern American families often shower their children with affection and brag about their achievements by doing such things as putting bumper stickers on their minivans that state such things as "My child is an honor student at . . ."; but in the 1930s the parent-child relationship was fundamentally different.

In the 1930s and actually until the 1960s, children were to be seen, not heard, and it was the parents' job to provide financially and socially for the children, which by all accounts the Heirens family did.

But William Heirens' inability to connect with others extended beyond his classmates or even his parents.

William was not very close with his younger brother either, although he was known to often fight his brother's battles against the neighborhood kids. The youngest Heirens would sometimes come back home with black eyes and a bloody nose, which William took as a personal affront. The older brother would charge out into the street and confront the neighborhood bullies – sometimes he would get the better of the bullies and other times he would limp back home as injured as his younger brother.

Young William showed a lack of fear and apparently also demonstrated a pain threshold that was much higher than that of other children his age. He was not known to cry or even complain when he fell, was hit by a ball, or even when other boys beat him up.

His high pain threshold was obviously a trait that set him apart from all the other kids his age and was one that kept the bullies at bay from him and eventually his younger brother.

Heirens' high pain threshold probably helped him become a good wrestler while he was in high school. At the time of his murder arrest, he was a well-built, athletic 159 pound young man who could have excelled in many sports, but his penchant for solitude prevented him from becoming any sort of notable athlete. He despised the very notion of team sports, which was an apparent reflection of his lack of empathy for society in general.

Young Heirens was an average student in grade school, although he showed an above average aptitude for mechanical skills. As a child, he fixed several radios and small engines and truly enjoyed taking things apart and putting them back together.

Alone, each of these traits – repressed sexuality, inability to connect with others, and a high pain threshold – are nothing spectacular, but when combined they paint the picture of a disturbed child whose only release was to dismember appliances and put them together again.

But as time went by, dismembering radios and motors was not enough for Heirens – he would move on to burglaries and eventually murder and dismemberment of a human.

CHAPTER 2:
Early Criminal Activity

William Heirens, like most serial killers, honed his criminal skills at an early age before he eventually graduated to murder. And like many other serial killers, Heirens' criminal activity was not driven by greed or survival but more so by lust. Not long after young Heirens' underwear fetish began, he started to commit burglaries. In terms of his skills as a burglar were concerned, Heirens displayed a particular aptitude as he claimed to have committed over 300 but was only caught on three occasions.

But when other boys his age were hanging out at the neighborhood soda fountain with their friends and chasing after girls for excitement, Heirens was breaking into people's homes for the sheer thrill.

As a delivery boy for a local pharmacy, Heirens had the perfect cover and opportunity for his crimes. After his normal day at school, he would report to his job at the pharmacy where he would deliver prescriptions, food, and other items to the store's customers. While in the customers' homes he would case them out, but not for items of value. Heirens main intent was to see how he would enter the home – if he needed to crawl in through a window with a ladder, which was his favorite mode of entry, or if he could enter through a door.

In particular, Heirens described the process of entering through a window as being especially stimulating as he told psychiatrists while he was being held in jail awaiting trial for murder. "Yes there was sexual excitement. I always had an erection."

Since Heirens' burglaries were lust driven and because his family was financially stable, the Lipstick Killer usually took things of little value, which often included women's underwear. There is no evidence that Heirens ever pawned items from his burglaries or tried to sell them to a fence. He was also not known to show any of his stolen items off to other kids at school or in the neighborhood. It was as if the items Heirens stole were his own little personal mementos of his victorious nights on the streets of Chicago.

Despite Heirens' penchant for burglaries, he knew that what he was doing was wrong, legally, if not morally. The burglaries created a dilemma for Heirens: on the one hand the burglaries were wrong, but on the other he felt compelled by some force to keep committing them.

Heirens tried to fight the force, but eventually it proved to be too much for the young man.

Walking through Darkness

Heirens later claimed that he tried to stop committing burglaries, but that the urge would get so great that he would eventually get a headache. The only way he found to relieve the headache was to go out and commit burglaries.

"When did the headaches come into the picture?" asked a psychiatrist. "When I tried to resist the urge to get outside and burglarize. It seemed as though I was in a dream. I did not have any feeling. It was like walking through darkness and pushing a mist aside," answered Heirens.

The surreal answer that Heirens gave to the psychiatrist was indicative of the world that the young man had built around himself. He was surrounded by darkness and the only way to escape was by breaking into people's homes.

But the burglaries proved to be no relief and Heirens continued to struggle with his criminal desires. He told psychiatrists that he eventually developed a method to stop the headaches, which was nominally successful.

"I would just put my hand on the table, then the headache would get too strong and I thought if I could just get out it would help. I had to get into any old thing. When I got these urges I would take out plans and draw how to get into certain places." Heirens said. "I would burn up the plans; sometimes they helped. I was playing a game with myself. I would draw up plans and then burn them or tear them up. I must have drawn about 500 plans on how to enter a house or rob a train or things of that sort."

Despite his self-treatment, Heirens was unable to quell his criminal urges. The headaches continued and he made more and more walks through the darkness.

Eventually though his walks became more brazen until the Chicago police caught up with him.

Heirens' First Arrest

Despite planning his burglaries quite well and possessing a particularly high aptitude for criminal endeavors, Heirens' first string of burglaries came to an end in June, 1942.

For the young William Heirens it was just another night on the streets of Chicago. He planned to go in through some windows, possibly steal some small items such as women's underwear, and then go home. The thefts were secondary, or even tertiary in purpose; his primary focus was to eliminate his headache and attain sexual stimulation and relief through the act of breaking and entering.

As he lurked around an apartment building on Chicago's north side, a concerned resident noticed the well-built stranger enter the building's basement storeroom. Heirens' pillaging of the basement fit the profile of his numerous other burglaries and also of the Suzanne Degnan murder over three years later.

Once the Chicago police responded to the call from the concerned neighbor they arrived at the apartment building and arrested Heirens for trespassing, but once they searched the young man the charges escalated as they discovered a concealed pistol on him.

Heirens was immediately detained and the police then searched the Heirens family home where they discovered a cache of stolen property and more weapons. Most of the stolen items the police found in the Heirens home were of little value and most perplexing to them was the large amount of women's underwear. In 1942, the discovery of a large amount of stolen women's underwear was for the most part written off and ignored as part of some type of "panty raid" or the workings of an inexperienced criminal.

Heirens was on no simple "panty raid" and he was far from an inexperienced criminal, even at the tender age of thirteen.

The local authorities quickly determined that Heirens' case was a bit more serious than a simple trespassing charge. The young Heirens was promptly arrested and entered into the system as a juvenile. After the authorities arrested Heirens, they quickly learned that he was not your average kid who broke into a home for thrills – he admitted to committing nine separate burglaries in the six months leading up to his arrest.

It was painfully obvious that William Heirens was not your average thirteen year old boy.

Reformatory Days

As part of his punishment, Heirens was sent to the Gibault School in Terre Haute, Indiana in order to learn life skills and pay his penance for his crimes. The Gibault School was much different than many other juvenile facilities in the United States at the time, or even today, in that the focus truly was on rehabilitation and the facility was not known for violence.

There is no evidence to suggest that Heirens was either the victim or perpetrator of violence on other kids while he was incarcerated at the Gibault School. Heirens and all of the other boys who were there were given access to basic high school education and vocational trade classes were available. Heirens' family also supported him through the sentence, which lasted from July 5, 1942 until June 4, 1943, by writing him letters and he was even employed at his father's company when he obtained a furlough in the summer of 1943, just before his official release.

"I was glad you stuck by me then," wrote Heirens to his parents in 1946 concerning his juvenile incarceration. "Nobody else did & nobody seemed to want to help. You didn't leave me or talk against me as other people did. You've stood by me & I cannot forget that. I know I didn't deserve it."

For many young men the time away from family and the lack of freedom that comes with incarceration would have been a wakeup call, but Heirens was not an ordinary young man. Something different drove William.

Heirens even related in a letter to his parents that was written from the Cook County Jail while he was awaiting trial for murder that his time at the reformatory was misspent and actually helped him become a better criminal. Heirens wrote:

"Then I was sent to Gibault. It probable was a mistake on the judges part because it didn't help me any. I picked up more about burglary & I got great excitement just talking about it. At first at Gibault I felt very sorry. You'll never know how many nights I cried myself to sleep. I tried at first to turn my thoughts to studies but later I guess I just drifted back to the same ideas."

After Heirens was released in the summer of 1943 he returned to live with his parents in Chicago and appeared at first glance to be reformed: he continued to work part time and enrolled in school.

Heirens knew how to say the right things to the people that mattered and he was able to develop the façade of a normal, all-American teen. In retrospect, Heirens was just developing the skills that most serial killers employ during their killing careers – the intangible ability to manipulate people and situations around them in order to deflect any suspicion away from their nefarious activities. With that said, the façade can only last as long as one is able to evade the police.

Shortly after his release from juvenile hall, Heirens continued "going out at night" burglarizing homes on Chicago's north side; but in his own words, things were much worse than before.

"When I left Gibault for home I came back worst than I started. I had plans & in the middle of the summer I went back to the same thing. I got great excitement out of it all. Then I was caught again. At Gibault, I learned very many things but it seemed none of them could stop me from stealing," wrote Heirens to his parents in 1946.

Just two months after his release from the Gibault School, Heirens was arrested for burglary once more. The urges proved too be much for Heirens despite the fact that he was on the police radar for his string of burglaries in 1942. Any burglary that matched Heirens' method of operation meant that he would be a suspect in the crime – young William Heirens painted himself into a criminal corner!

For Heirens' second stretch in a juvenile facility, he was sent to Saint Bede's Academy in Peru, Illinois. Saint Bede's, like the Gibault School, was a Catholic institution. In particular, Saint Bede's was administered by the Benedictine order, which meant that Heirens received an ample amount of religious education to go along with the high school classes he took while incarcerated. For the standard of the time, Saint Bede's was much more dedicated to rehabilitating and educating its young men than in punishing them.

The social situation at Saint Bede's also appears to have been similar to that at the Gibault School: there is no indication that violence was a major part of his time there and he was given another furlough in the summer of 1944 to return to Chicago in order to work with his father.

While Heirens was incarcerated at Saint Bede's, he made the most of his time and once more put on a good façade for his family and the authorities.

But as a letter written to his parents in 1946 demonstrates, even the lighter hand of Saint Bede's was not enough to steer Heirens on the righteous path.

"I started my second year at St. Bede with the money from the steel mills. I hated to go back I wanted the normal schooling being able to see you after school & getting around with regular guys," wrote Heirens. "The last year at St. Bede my mind began to wander again as it did at Gibault. I had very few things to occupy it & I began to feel you didn't want me at home. I planned how I would do more burglaries. At that time I got a lot of excitement in planning such things. Then summer came again & I felt still that you didn't care about me so I wanted to get out on my own & prove that I was not a baby & I wanted to show you there was some good in me."

A Most Precocious Sociopath

Serial killers are a diverse lot when one examines their various pathologies, methodologies, and backgrounds. Some killers, such as Donald Henry Gaskins and Henry Lee Lucas, came from low income backgrounds and were barely literate, while others, like Ted Bundy, saw themselves as intellectually superior to others and sometimes sought to prove as much by embarking on academic endeavors. When viewed from this perspective, William Heirens shared some similarities with Bundy.

Psychiatrists determined that Heirens possessed an average IQ, but the young man seemed to be driven to prove that he was intellectually superior to most people.

Heirens certainly had the ambition to accompany his intellectual delusions.

The future Lipstick Killer did not let either of his juvenile incarcerations slow the progress of his education and in fact he graduated high school early at the age of sixteen while at Saint Bede's Academy.

Upon his high school graduation, Heirens set out to realize his goals of intellectual superiority by applying and ultimately being accepted to the prestigious University of Chicago.

Shortly after he was accepted to the University of Chicago, Heirens wrote some of his thoughts on the situation in a notebook, which was later confiscated by the police after his murder arrest. The tone of the note is for the most part down to earth, but there is a slight sense of grandiosity.

"My hopes and prayers have been answered in one of my biggest chances in life. I can only use my chance to the best advantage. The University of Chicago has accepted me into its enrollment. This is my first chance at showing how good I am to society and I intend to show even better signs. Tonight I feel as if the world were mine. All I have to do now is pray, giving thanks and vowing to do my best as humanly possible," wrote Heirens.

Heirens enrolled at the University of Chicago in September, 1945 and remained there until he was arrested for murder nearly one year later. In his year of academic studies he took general education requirements, but majored in electrical engineering. Again, he was drawn to taking things apart in order to see how they worked.

But academic pursuits would not be enough to placate the troubled young William Heirens. The headaches came back and he eventually succumbed to walk through the darkness once more.

CHAPTER 3:
The Murder Spree

Compared to other notable serial killers, William Heirens' career was much shorter and less prolific. Some killers, such as Bundy, Gaskins, and Lucas, hunted humans for years and left scores or more of victims in their wake. Heirens' serial killer career only took place over a less than seven month period and he only claimed three victims.

Some experts may even claim that Heirens does not fit the definition of a serial killer. The FBI, whose agents first coined the term "serial killer," defines a serial killer as one who, either alone or with an accomplice, kills at least three people over a period of time with a "cooling off" period between murders. Heirens was convicted of three murders, but whether there was a "cooling off" period between murders is open for debate. There was a sixth month period between Heirens' first and second murders, but less than a month between the second and third.

Regardless of whether or not Heirens should be classified as a serial killer or a spree killer, his repressed sexual thoughts and feelings of superiority were manifested in a fury of homicidal rage on June 5, 1945.

The Murder of Josephine Ross

Josephine Ross was a single, 43 year old Chicagoan who was found stabbed to death in her apartment on the north side of Chicago at 4108 North Kenmore in the warm summer of 1945. She was known to be a friendly, vivacious woman who had no known enemies. Her fiancé and ex-boyfriends all had solid alibis for the time of her murder, which left the Chicago police and the citizens of the Windy City confused and in fear.

Who would kill such an innocent person?

When the details of Ross' murder began to slowly emerge in the press, then the public became even more concerned.

She was stabbed multiple times and although she had not been raped, there were signs that the killer spent considerable time in her apartment before, during, and after the murder!

Bandages were found wrapped around the sliced throat of Ross, as if the killer had attempted to save her. There were also signs that the killer masturbated in different places throughout the apartment, either during or after the homicidal act. Ross' lifeless body clutched a clump of dark hair, which meant that she had fought for her life.

This was a new type of killer that the people of Chicago, or the United States, were not accustomed to, as it appeared to be the work of a sexually demented "thrill killer." The people of Chicago began to lock their doors and keep weapons close at hand. No one knew where the maniac would strike next.

The Chicago Police Department dedicated extra resources to finding Ross' killer: they canvassed the neighborhood looking for physical evidence and searched their records for any known criminals that worked under a similar method of operation. In the end, the only evidence police were able to gather were witness reports of a man with dark hair and complexion who was lurking around the apartment building before the murder.

Ultimately, the clump of hair that Josephine Ross clutched in her hand proved to be more fodder for the press than it was evidence for the police. Since DNA identification was still decades away from being a reality and was not even a thought in 1945, the hair only helped to narrow down the field of potential suspects.

William Heirens had dark hair.

Heirens later told investigators and psychiatrists that he never intended to kill Ross, only to rob her apartment, but that when she screamed when she saw him come in through the window he was compelled to kill her.

Heirens claimed that he felt nothing – good or bad – other than he was afraid of being caught. After he went home for the night, he slept as soundly as any other night.

Heirens had let the murderous Pandora out its box – more carnage was soon to follow.

The Frances Brown Murder

After a "cool down" period of just over six months, Heirens struck again, killing another innocent woman. Frances Brown was found stabbed and shot to death in her apartment on the north side of Chicago at 3941 North Pine Grove on December 11, 1945, murdered in a similar manner as Josephine Ross – stabbed and mutilated several times.

But the Francis Brown murder was different because the killer left a message.

"Heavens sake catch me before I kill more I cannot control myself" was scrawled, in notably poor grammar, in lipstick on the wall of Brown's apartment. The police were left scratching their heads once more as they asked who would kill this woman and why would the killer leave such a bizarre, enigmatic message?

Frances Brown, like Josephine Ross, was an unlikely murder victim. She was not involved in drug use, drinking, or any criminal activity and she was not known to go out with many men. In fact, Brown was the prototypical all-American woman who had just returned from military service in World War II.

The case not only perplexed the police, it frightened the public, especially once a connection was made with the Ross murder and the contents of the lipstick message were revealed by the press. The message itself became fodder for themes in later movies and television shows such as *Alfred Hitchcock Presents* and *Thriller*; but on a forensic level it represented one of the first pieces of hard evidence that would later link Heirens to the string of murders he committed.

It was not the only evidence Heirens left at the scene.

The Chicago police also lifted a bloody fingerprint from a door jamb and the desk clerk who was working the night of the murder witnessed a "nervous looking man" leave the building around the time of the killing.

All of this evidence would later be used to send Heirens to prison for the rest of his life, but what was more interesting and disturbing, was the confessed details of the crime the killer later gave to psychiatrists.

"Going in I had an erection. When I realized what was going on, I was in the living room sitting in a chair," related Heirens on his felonious entry into Brown's apartment. When the psychiatrists asked why he killed Brown he simply answered, "Just to keep her quiet."

After the murder, Heirens retreated to the safety of his dorm room on the University of Chicago campus where he enjoyed a good night's sleep.

"Did you read about it in the paper?" asked the psychiatrists. "Yes," responded Heirens. "How did you feel when you read about it in the paper?" continued the line of questioning. "Just like anything else in the paper. It did not bother me," answered Heirens.

Heirens definitely displayed the most common trait that all serial killers share – a lack of empathy – in this and other interviews he had with the psychiatrists. Although Heirens felt no empathy for his first two victims, he also apparently took no real joy in the murders. He claimed that they were committed for utilitarian purposes; because the women screamed as he broke into their apartments.

For Heirens' third and last known murder, he brought his killing to a whole new level, one where he seems to have reveled in his sadism and brutality.

The Kidnapping, Murder, and Dismemberment of Suzanne Degnan

As the first week in 1946 ended, the Degnan family was grateful for the blessings of the previous year and looked forward to an equally enjoyable and productive 1946. They had a nice family and their home was one of the nicest in the neighborhood. It was a modest two story brownstone on the north side at 5943 North Kenmore.

Unfortunately for them it was on the same street where Josephine Ross was killed and directly in the middle of the Lipstick Killer's hunting grounds.

On January 7, 1946, while the city of Chicago was still reeling from the brutal Ross and Brown murders, the parents of six year old Suzanne Degnan discovered that their little girl was not sleeping in her room as she should have been. The hysterical parents frantically searched every inch of their house to no avail. Their daughter was missing.

The Degnans quickly called the Chicago police who rapidly responded to the call. Even in those years long before Amber Alerts, a missing child was taken very seriously. At first the police thought that the little girl had probably just wandered off for a bit or was playing a trick on her parents by hiding somewhere; but their optimism soon turned to dread when they did a search of the house and the surrounding area.

A ladder was found outside of Suzanne's window, which told the investigators that the girl was probably abducted. A further search of the premises confirmed their suspicions when they found what appeared to be a poorly written ransom note.

"Get $20,000 ready and waite for word. Do not notify FBI or police. Bills in $5's and $10's," was scrawled in poorly written and spelled grammar on one side while on the other it stated, "Burn this note for her safty."

Defenders of Heirens have pointed out that Heirens was fairly intelligent and probably would not have written a note of such poor grammatical quality; but investigators later argued that he consciously wrote the note so poorly in order to throw police off on a wild goose chase. It should also be pointed out that although Heirens did fairly well in his engineering classes in college, he failed English once in high school. One can also see from the letters Heirens wrote to his parents and girlfriend from the county jail in 1946 that his spelling and grammar had not improved much since his high school days. The note was also written at the scene and in a panic and he therefore had no time to proof it for spelling and grammatical errors.

Despite confirming that their daughter had indeed been kidnapped, the Degnans held out hope that their daughter was still alive and that the kidnapper, or kidnappers, was only after money and would return her once paid.

The problem was that the kidnapper never left any further instructions or how he could be reached. The Degnans were forced to wait for the kidnapper to make the next move.

Shortly after the abduction, the kidnapper began calling the Degnan household demanding the ransom, but would always hang up before any meaningful details, such as a drop location, were related. In retrospect, this behavior was clearly in-line with that of many other serial killers since police later determined that Suzanne was dead when the phone calls took place. Heirens was merely playing a game with the victim's family by demonstrating the power he had over them.

According to later psychiatric interviews with the Lipstick Killer, he killed and dismembered Suzanne Degnan immediately after abducting her from the home. He dismembered her body in the basement of a nearby apartment building at 5901 North Winthrop and then scattered her body parts in the sewers.

Heirens made one last phone call to the police and told them to search the sewers behind the Degnan's apartment.

The police took the call seriously and conducted a search in the area, which resulted in the discovery of Suzanne Degnan's dismembered body parts. It seems that Heirens took his interest of disassembling things in order to see how they work and applied it to humans.

The young Lipstick Killer had clearly graduated to the level of a sadistic serial killer.

Heirens later told investigators that after he had dismembered Degnan with a hunting knife, he went back to his dorm room, ate two breakfasts, and then attended classes all day.

Again, he felt nothing.

Reasons for Murder?

The vast majority of humans, apart from acts of self-defense, find few if any justifiable reasons to take another human's life.

The very thought of murder is detestable to most and the act tears at the very fabric of civilized society. Since the beginning of human civilization over 5,000 years ago, laws have been codified that dictate severe punishments for taking a human life.

Most people never have to be told killing is wrong since empathy is a trait common to most humans. But for people like William Heirens and other serial killers murder is something they do to achieve a certain end, or even for fun.

Heirens was later asked by psychiatrists what his reasons were for killing his three victims.

"On three occasions you were surprised by people seeing you and you immediately killed. Why did you do that?" asked a psychiatrist. "It was the noise that set me off, I believe. I must have been in a high tension and the least bit of noise would disturb me in that manner," responded Heirens.

A normal person would not kill someone because of a noise; but then again, a normal person does not break into hundreds of residences and get sexually stimulated in the process.

William Heirens was far from a normal person.

Other Suspects

Although the Suzanne Degnan kidnapping and murder captured most of the attention from the police and media in the days and weeks following the discovery of her dismembered body, the murders of Ross and Brown were not forgotten. Police had linked the Ross and Brown murders to the same perpetrator, but had not yet placed Degnan's murder in the series. The police frantically searched their files for any convicted killers, child molesters, and thieves who fit the method of operation and they also scoured the Degnan's neighborhood for any witnesses.

The police very quickly got their first suspect.

Victor Verburgh was a sixty five year old janitor who worked in the building where the Degnan's lived. Verburgh had no criminal record, but was an immigrant who kept to himself and he had access to both the building and the place where police believed Suzanne was killed, so he became their prime suspect.

Verburgh was picked up and brought to the central police station in downtown Chicago where he was then "questioned."

1946 was long before the *Miranda* rule came into effect and also well before cameras and the American Civil Liberties Union were there to keep police honest, which meant that interrogations could sometimes approach a medieval level. In Verburgh's case that is exactly what happened.

Verburgh was held at police headquarters for two days and allowed no contact with a lawyer or any family members. Over the course of the forty eight hours he was repeatedly beaten and threatened with even greater violence unless he confessed to Suzanne Degnan's murder. Verburgh never relented and finally lawyers from the janitor's union that he belonged to had him released on a writ of *habeas corpus*.

After Verburgh was released from police custody, he then spent ten days in the county hospital recovering from wounds he sustained during his interrogation. He later sued the Chicago Police Department and won $20,000, which was a considerable chunk of change in those days.

When Verburgh turned out to be a dead end in the Degnan murder investigation, the Chicago police quickly focused on a new suspect. During the search of the Degnan residence, a handkerchief with the monogram "S. Sherman" was discovered. Investigators surmised that it was similar to handkerchiefs that were popular with servicemen at the time so they conducted an exhaustive search of military records for any name that fit the monogram.

Most people do not think of Chicago as a military town and per capita it is not, but the primary navy basic training facility is located in nearby North Chicago. Thousands of sailors and marines pass through training every year at the facility and many take their weekend liberties in the city of Chicago. Throughout the history of the facility, things have been run fairly well and most Chicagoans look at the base as an asset to the community; but as with anything else, a bad apple can spoil the whole barrel.

Investigators began to think that the perpetrator of Suzanne Degnan's murder may have been a sailor or marine on weekend liberty who had too much drink and for some reason decided to act on some unnatural violent impulse.

The Chicago police learned that a marine named Sidney Sherman had the same initials as those on the handkerchief and that he had left Chicago shortly after the Degnan murder.

A nationwide search for Sidney Sherman quickly found the young marine days later in Toledo, Ohio where he had just eloped with his girlfriend. The suspect was brought back to Chicago, questioned, and given a polygraph exam in which he was determined to be truthful.

Sidney Sherman was eliminated as a suspect and the owner of the handkerchief was never found. Investigators later determined that the handkerchief was a red herring and was not related to the murder in any way.

Finally, two more suspects emerged after they inserted themselves into the situation.

Theodore Campbell and Vincent Costello were two Chicago teenagers like William Heirens. And like William Heirens, Campbell and Costello were both aspiring criminals.

Campbell and Costello liked to wear leather jackets, roll their jeans up, smoke cigarettes, and carry switchblade knives. The two juvenile delinquents also enjoyed skipping school, getting into fights, running with local street gangs, and committing petty crimes.

Campbell and Costello also lived in the Degnan's neighborhood.

The difference between Campbell and Costello and Heirens though seemed to be clearly along the lines of IQ. Heirens, although no genius, was relatively intelligent while Campbell and Costello were clearly a few cards short of a deck.

The two quickly learned of Suzanne Degnan's abduction and before her body was recovered, formulated a get rich quick scheme.

The two bumbling fools decided to call the Degnan family with ransom demands.

According to the police, the calls placed by the duo were barely coherent and displayed an obvious lack of organization. Humored by the stunt, Campbell began to boast about the call to other local delinquents on Chicago's north side until one with a conscience turned him in to the police. The Chicago police quickly apprehended Campbell, who then just as promptly turned in his cohort. After some cursory questioning, the police began to suspect that neither had anything to do with the murder and after the two were given a polygraph examination it was determined that they did not.

The police had run out of suspects and the city of Chicago was on edge.

CHAPTER 4:
The Nightmare Ends

The investigation of Suzanne Degnan's murder needs to be placed in the context of its time. The murder took place long before the National Crime Information Center (NCIC) database or the Integrated Automated Fingerprint Identification System (IAFIS) were created and before the use of criminal profilers by police departments became common place. With that said, as discussed above, police were given much more leeway in their interrogation of suspects and searches of their persons and properties.

None of that seemed to matter – the Lipstick Killer was like a ghost, a phantom who crept through the shadows of Chicago's brownstone homes and apartments.

But sometimes a cop's best tool is good old fashioned luck!

The Arrest

The three murders that Heirens committed did not slow down his nocturnal burglary sprees throughout the city of Chicago. Despite later claiming that the murders were all incidental and the result of having to silence his victims, Heirens showed no remorse or a desire to turn himself into the authorities.

The Lipstick killer continued to take classes at the University of Chicago during the day and then burglarize homes and apartments at night, either on the south side near his dorm room, or on the north side near his parents' home.

He also made some half-hearted attempts to be a normal college student by attending social functions, trying to make friends, and even dated a few girls.

But the headaches returned and Heirens was compelled to walk through the darkness again and again as he burglarized several more homes.

Heirens used his dorm room at the University of Chicago as his criminal headquarters in this final spate of burglaries where he focused his activities more on the lake front south side instead of the north side where he committed his three murders. Besides changing location, Heirens began to get more brazen in his final series of thefts.

In April, Heirens was arrested by the Chicago police for walking down the street on the south side near the campus of the University of Chicago with a loaded rifle.

After Heirens was brought into the police station, he quickly manipulated the situation to his advantage.

Heirens explained to the police officers that he was a student at the University of Chicago and that he was merely bringing the gun from a friend's house back to his dorm room. Heirens further pointed out that the gun was not concealed and therefore not illegal. The police were impressed with the articulate, knowledgeable young man and so dropped charges before he was ever officially charged.

Heirens would continue to burglarize homes in Chicago.

Finally, on June 26, 1946, Heirens burglarized the wrong apartment.

On the night in question Heirens was trolling his old hunting grounds, the north side, for homes to burglarize. He ended up in the Rogers Park neighborhood and found an apartment that appealed to him on North Wayne Street. Following his typical criminal routine, he lurked around an apartment building's basement and looked for an entrance into the dwelling. As he crept through the brownstone's basement, the apartment's maintenance man disrupted the killer's nefarious activities, which then led to a violent and frenzied chase.

Heirens quickly ran out of the apartment building's back basement door followed closely by the worker. Not wanting to be caught, Heirens turned around, pointed a gun at the man and exclaimed, "Let me get out or I'll let you have it in the guts!"

Not wanting to get shot, the man relinquished the chase and instead called the police.

Heirens did not get very far, just a couple of buildings away where he then sought refuge in another basement. The police quickly cordoned off the area as they sensed that they may have the Lipstick Killer. The details of the next chain of events diverge based on whose statement is considered.

The Chicago police claim that once they located Heirens, he pointed his pistol at them, pulled the trigger, and when the gun jamed he charged them. Heirens on the other hand claimed that he merely brandished the gun and then turned and ran in the opposite direction before being run down and cuffed by police officers.

The Lipstick Killer was finally in custody.

William Heirens in Custody

Once Heirens was in custody the legal case against him quickly picked up steam. Investigators believed that they not only had Suzanne Degnan's murderer, but also the killer of Frances Brown and Josephine Ross.

Heirens claimed he was beaten for six days and not allowed to see an attorney. Considering what the Chicago police did to Victor Verburgh, there is no reason not to believe this accusation, although that does not mean Heirens was innocent.

Perhaps not wanting to revisit the Verburgh fiasco, investigators subjected Heirens to a treatment of sodium pentothal – often referred to as the "truth serum" – without a lawyer present or the consent of his parents, as he was just shy of his eighteenth birthday at the time. The legality and practicality of Heirens' sodium pentothal treatment were later brought into question, which will be explored more below, but at the time it was believed to be a good practice and solid evidence of guilt or innocence.

During the treatment, Heirens never admitted to the three murders but eluded to the possible involvement of his murderous alter ego, "George Murman."

The Polygraph Examination

Heirens, like all of the other suspects in the murders, was also subjected to a polygraph examination. The polygraph's legality was also later called into question, as results are not admissible in American courts, but interestingly Heirens' came back inconclusive.

Investigators concluded that polygraph examinations could be "beat" at times and that Heirens did so because of his lack of remorse and feeling for his victims.

It did not take long for the local and then the national press to get hold of the Heirens case. In many ways the case was just made for the press: a young killer who could have done much more with his life, a city on edge over his crimes, and the crimes themselves, especially Degnan's murder, which were just too much for many people in 1946 American to comprehend.

It was also the press that gave Heirens the nickname the Lipstick Killer.

The Press Gets Involved

As Heirens sat in the Cook County Jail awaiting trial, the case became a spectacle; but the lurid details of the murders and why Heirens committed them were also revealed.

A study conducted on the media's treatment of the Lipstick Killer case counted 387 stories on the case in eighty five issues over just an eighteen day period. The same study determined that the case accounted for the headline story in 73% of issues while it was ongoing.

The rush to publish stories about the Heirens case was driven by a combination of the papers' need to meet the demands of their readers, the desire by journalists to get coveted bylines, and intense competition between the papers.

Sometimes the result was inaccurate reporting and elements of "yellow journalism."

The *Chicago Tribune* led the charge to the point that other local and national papers often reprinted, word for word, the articles of from the *Tribune*.

Also, as will be discussed below, reporters often inserted themselves directly into the investigation, which today would call into question the journalist's objectivity and threaten to contaminate evidence and possibly the entire case against the defendant.

CHAPTER 5:
Awaiting Trial

For most criminal defendants who are awaiting trial on a felony charge in the United States justice system, the option of bail is given. Depending on the circumstances and severity of the crime, the bail may be quite high or relatively low; Heirens was denied bail for the particularly egregious nature of the crime and the fact that he made a confession days after his arrest.

Also, most defendants awaiting trial spend their days in boredom, waiting for their preliminary hearing dates and meeting with their lawyers. Since Heirens was a high profile inmate, his days were spent under the glare of the press as he met with his legal team. Heirens was given a court appointed team of attorneys who requested an examination by a team of psychiatrists.

The lawyers believed that since their client confessed to the crimes and there appeared to be a mountain of forensic evidence stacked against him, the psychiatrists would find Heirens insane and he would thereby be sent to a mental hospital instead of a tough Illinois prison. Initially, Heirens did feign insanity, but that façade quickly crumbled once the examination was conducted.

The examination was conducted in the chapel of the Cook County Jail for six hour sessions over a span of nearly three weeks by Foster Kennedy, Harry R. Hoffman, and William H. Haines.

The psychiatrists determined that Heirens possessed an IQ of 110 and that he was deeply disturbed, although legally sane.

The interviews uncovered the pathology that drove the Lipstick Killer, as well as his criminal methodology.

Dr. Jekyll and Mr. Hyde

One of the most illuminating parts of the interview is when Heirens was asked if there were any movies that he enjoyed particularly. He answered that in 1942 he went to see *Dr. Jekyll and Mr. Hyde* and that the movie had a profound impact on his life. He said that the movie seemed to speak to him and that it was if the movie reflected his own life. It was at this point that Heirens opened up the psychiatrists about his murderous alter ego, George Murman.

"He came into the picture before I started to burglarize in 1942," said Heirens to the doctors. "In the beginning I always tried to resist and after that I tried to talk to him, and later on developed writing to him."

The doctors continued to prod Heirens for answers about George: was he the result of some trauma or was he just made up?

"He was just a realization of mine. I just struck him in for no good reason. Before he seemed real to me," answered Heirens.

Insanity or Hoax?

Multiple personality disorder is well known among mental health professionals, but most people afflicted with the disorder rarely resort to violence, so some believe that Heirens concocted George Murman in order to obtain an insanity defense.

The case of another famous American serial killer over thirty years later may point to Heirens elaborate creation of his alter ego.

In the late 1970s, Los Angeles, California was gripped with fear when several women were abducted and murdered by what the press called the "Hillside Strangler." The Hillside Strangler actually turned out to be two men, Kenneth Bianchi and Angelo Buono. In 1980, while Bianchi was awaiting trial in the state of Washington for the murder of two more women, he feigned multiple personality disorder by claiming that his murderous alter ego, "Steve Walker," made him commit the murders. Although he initially persuaded a psychiatrist that he suffered from the disorder, further interviews and investigation revealed that it was all a charade Bianchi invented in order to win an insanity plea.

The psychiatrists that examined Heirens never determined if he suffered from multiple personality disorder or if it was an elaborate hoax he cooked up, but elements of the interview can point to either being the case.

Throughout the interviews, Heirens repeatedly used the word "vague" to describe how he remembered his criminal activities and how he interacted with his alter ego.

"At Gibalt things were so vague when I went out on burglary, it seemed to me that George was doing it. He seemed to be real. I cannot introduce him to anybody but he is there," said the Lipstick Killer.

The psychiatrists took issue with Heirens use of the word "vague."

"I object to your general statement that 'things were so vague," responded one of the doctors to Heirens. "You are not using the right term. Maybe they were 'different' but not 'vague.' For instance, in the Degnan case, you were able to see there was somebody sleeping on the right hand side by your flash light. You saw that somebody sitting up and that she had long hair, and you were able to see that somebody begin to talk and you answered. You also saw that the door on the other side of the room was shut," the psychiatrist then continued. "You took the child and went out the window. Your word 'vague' is wrong. You were in an unusual condition, but not 'vague.'"

Over the course of the psychological examination, Heirens related yet more details as to how George compelled him to commit crimes, particularly how the events would begin.

"Usually when I had to get out I would ask him where he was going. We would talk back and forth that way. He would say, down to the lake, and I would say, what are you going to do there? He said he would get some things. I would ask him why he was going and he said, because he wants to. It would just be that way," explained Heirens.

The doctors asked Heirens if he tried to fight the urges, or to fight with George in order to not commit any more crimes.

"I would argue with him to stay and then I would get a headache," answered Heirens. "I would argue in every way possible with him but he always wanted to get out."

As the psychologists continued to question Heirens about his alter ego, they quickly learned that George allowed Heirens to do other things that he normally could not. It was if Heirens believed George was imbued with super powers.

When asked about his flight from the police on June 26, 1946 Heirens said: "At the time I had the power of George I could run faster than anyone. I should have kept running. I went into a back alley and upstairs and asked a lady for a drink of water."

"What did you tell her?" asked a psychiatrist.

"I said I had a heart attack. Then I came to myself, realized what had happened, and then the police started coming," responded Heirens.

The transcripts of the interview appear to reveal Heirens as a deeply disturbed, if not mentally ill young man; but the real possibility remains that he invented George in order to successfully land an insanity defense. At first glance it seems that the character is too complex and intricate for a young man to make up in a short time, but the case of Kenneth Bianchi presents another interesting parallel.

While Bianchi tried to pursue an insanity defense in his case, prosecutors discovered a plethora of psychological literature in his cell, some of which pertained specifically to multiple personality disorder. Apparently Bianchi did his homework.

Could William Heirens have done something similar?

Although no books on the subjects of psychology or psychiatric research were found in his cell in the county jail, the transcripts from his psychological examination reveals that he had an interest in and knowledge of current research in the field.

"What subjects are you interested in?" asked the doctors.

"I am interested in psychology as far as that goes," answered Heirens.

The doctors then pressed the Lipstick Killer further and asked if he considered his serial burglary spree normal for a boy his age.

"You don't think there is anything about you different from the average boy 13 to 17?"

"Just going out nights, that's all," quipped Heirens.

The doctors took exception with Heirens' perfunctory answer.

"You account for it with euphemisms," stated one of the psychiatrists. "You couldn't account for it, and you didn't seek any advice in any way?"

"I sought advice by reading," replied Heirens. After the psychiatrists asked him what he read he stated: "Around the subject of masochism, fetishism, sadism, flagellation."

With their interest piqued, the doctors asked where he read about those subject, which Heirens answered by stating he read a lot of the nineteenth century German psychiatrist, Richard von Kraft-Ebbing's works.

To be fair, simply having read some psychiatric titles does not mean that Heirens made up the alter ego of George in order to win an insanity defense, but it does demonstrate that he had an advanced knowledge of the subject.

After all, how many seventeen year old boys read obscure nineteenth century German psychiatrists for fun?

In a letter to his parents written while he was in the county jail, Heirens claimed that he made up George during the sodium pentothal treatment.

"I then planned other things to lead to my conviction & eventually the electric chair," Heirens wrote. "I was too nervous when they used the truth serum for it to have any effect but when they started to question me I decided to play along & so I wanted to agravate them against me so I blamed it all on George M.S. of whom I had composed a note concerning. That all worked very well but I think I should have told them I did it in the truth serum."

Interestingly, despite giving Heirens a polygraph test, an interview under the influence of sodium pentothal, and several hours of in-depth examinations by three reputable psychiatrists, the authorities never bothered to interview him under hypnosis. When Bianchi was put under hypnosis by neutral doctors, it was soon revealed that he had made up the whole charade.

The doctors who examined Heirens determined that he possessed "a definite emotional insensitivity and instability severe enough to be considered abnormal, as well as a blunting of moral concepts," but that he was sane.

Heirens was a sociopath, clear and simple.

Mom and Dad

While Heirens was being held in the county jail he wrote a number of letters to his parents and at least one to a girl he dated. The tone of the letters, which often focused on his sexuality, can best be described as bizarre. The authorities intercepted all of his letters for potential evidence to be used against him at his murder trials, but he never admitted to any of the murders.

He did admit to his string of burglaries.

In one letter he connected his sexual perversions and repression with his desire to commit burglaries: "I therefore thought it must be something to do with sex so I deduced that the best way to overcome it was to get at the source which I did by dating girls. I found them repulsive but I was determined to overcome this. My burglaries were very frequent at the time & usually when I went out I committed more than one a night. But soon after Christmas when I started to go with Joan I began to let up on burglaries & I decided I was winning but I still made infrequent burglaries. I knew I was winning. Yet I had not overcome it. During the burglaries I had an erection either way in the place I burglarized so I decided to elevate any chances of more burglaries would be to go to the bathroom frequently before night & the urge I couldn't control would come on again. This also helped but not sufficiently. Joan was converting me away from my crime but not sufficiently. We never went further than necking & maybe that's the reason. Some houses I broke into I merely excreted in & left so I should say my total burglaries were vast considering the amount of things I stole & threw away."

Heirens then shifted gears and appeared much more normal in another part of the letter where he reflected on one of the better memories he had with his father and brother, perhaps because he knew that he would never see them again.

"Remember dad, when we went to work togeather during the summer. We'de get up early & go out to the care when the sun was just coming up. It sure was great. I guess I have the best father in the world. You would let me drive part of the way & I remember how you would be on pins and needles worrying about me hitting something. I thought that was funny that you should worry about me doing that. Yes, you are the greatest dad in the world. I remember when we'de go fishing real early in the morning. You & Jere always had a hard time getting me up. Then we would go down to the rocks on Lake Michigan & fish. Remember when we arrived it would still be dark & we'de get all the fish when the sun started to come up. I know I'll remember that. You were swell dad. There aren't many fathers that would do that much for their sun."

It remains to be seen if the content of the letter was truly heartfelt or just another manipulative ploy by Heirens in order to get something.

Heirens also wrote an equally strange letter to his girlfriend Joan, who he mentioned in the letter to his parents. Heirens appeared apologetic for involving her inadvertently in the case, but also seems to imply that he needed her as an alibi: "Dear Joan, I noticed your name in the New World last Sunday. When I think that mine might have been there with the rest it gives me a funny feeling & hate for myself that I cannot expressed. I hope the convention turns out alright. It looks like I won't have a date with you for that formal dance. I'm sorry about breaking it.

You'll never realize what I've been through. It all seems like a bad dream & I can't wake up. Every thing that the police can say to hurt me in any way they tell the newspapers. I want you to know that what is being said is not true. I never had anything to do with the Degnan case or all those burglaries & assaults. It seems the police are trying to say I did everything bad in Chicago but it isn't true, not a bit of it. . .

Quite a few times I spoke to you of knowing shady characters & now you can understand I wasn't telling a story. [I would hold thing for George, He is one of my friends the best I thought.] But it's all water under the bridge now [& George is a very far ways from Chicago] & I know something will come up help my case.

You can help me very much if you remember all the nights you & that we went out together [the best that you can remember].

Joan, I guess you know now that I never went out with many girls. I want you to know that I think very much of you, more than I ever did concerning girls. I couldn't avoid all the bother the police gave you even if I tried. It seems they poke their nose in everything. All I can do is wait for the truth to shine through to the public eye. I'll never forget you, Joan, No matter where you are I'll write & tell you what's happening. . .

I'll write again soon. If you have time drop me a few words will you. I never know what's in the newspaper or how the public is thinking here but be careful what you write because they change words around & use them as evidents against me. So for safety sake don't write anything concerning my case to me."

Heirens was correct; the letters were used as evidence against him in court. They demonstrated his propensity to lie, as he admitted to the burglaries to his parents, while he denied them in the letter to Joan. They definitely paint the picture of a confused, troubled, yet manipulative young man who seemed to be in control of his faculties.

The ability to lie is also a sign of an anti-social personality, which was essentially how the psychiatrists diagnosed Heirens.

But his confessions and the letters were not the only evidence the prosecutors used against Heirens.

Other Evidence

Heirens' confessions during the psychiatric examination, and the letters to his parents would have been enough to secure a conviction in an Illinois court in 1946, but there were a number of other pieces that came together to firmly point the finger at Heirens as the Lipstick Killer.

Most of the evidence that pointed toward Heirens' guilt was circumstantial, but even in the forensic obsessed world of today, people are routinely convicted of murder with circumstantial evidence if enough exists. In Heirens' case, the evidence was a combination of eye witness testimony, circumstantial evidence found in his possession, and some forensic evidence.

The forensic evidence against Heirens was not very solid by today's standards, but police claimed it provided tangible verification that he was at the scene of two of the three murders.

The only fingerprints that police were able to pull from any of the three murder scenes was a partial bloody finger print from a door jamb at Frances Brown's apartment. Despite it being just a partial print, police claimed that it was a match to Heirens. The police also argued that a fingerprint on the ransom note left behind after the Degnan murder matched Heirens' on nine points of comparison. Heirens argued in the decades after he was incarcerated that the comparison was not valid since the FBI was using a system that required twelve points of comparison in order to arrive at a positive identification. A positive identification of the lipstick message scrawled on the wall of Brown's apartment could not be made.

Along with the fingerprint evidence was a plethora of stolen items that police recovered from Heirens' dorm room and the home of his parents.

The police seized the cache of stolen property in warrantless searches that were later challenged by Heirens on appeal. Among some of the more bizarre items taken was a collection of Nazi memorabilia. Police quickly learned that the Third Reich items belonged to World War II veteran Henry Gold, who lived in the neighborhood of the Degnans. The police also learned that Gold's house was burglarized the same night as the Degnan murder, which put Heirens in the neighborhood doing what he did best – breaking into people's homes.

Another compelling bit of circumstantial evidence that worked against Heirens was the proximity of the murders to each other, his known burglary hunting grounds, and where he was arrested. Heirens admitted to burglarizing hundreds of homes and apartments, many on the north side of Chicago, which made him responsible for the overwhelming percentage of the crime in the neighborhood at that time. This is actually one piece of evidence that would be more damning against him today than it was in 1946.

Today, researchers can use sophisticated mapping software to depict where and when crime takes place. If investigators had access to such software in 1946 they would have been able to graphically demonstrate that not only was Heirens a one man crime wave on the north side of Chicago, but that the chances of another criminal entering the mix and committing three murders in his territory would have been remote.

The police also recovered a stolen medical kit, complete with knives and scalpels, in Heirens' possession. 1946 was over forty years before DNA testing became commonplace in criminal investigations, but investigators did have the ability to test for blood. Investigators determined that there was no evidence of biological material on the medical tools, or Heirens' clothing. With that said, the kit was further evidence of his burglary spree and a most curious item that did not help Heirens' later pleas of innocence.

Of all the stolen items found under the possession of Heirens, the pistol that he was carrying the night he was arrested was perhaps the most damning. According to police, the revolver was stolen from the home of a man named Guy Rodrick on the night of December 3, 1945. Two nights later, the gun was used to fire randomly into the apartment of Marion Caldwell, which resulted in a non-life threatening wound to the woman. After Heirens was arrested and the gun he had was tested, police determined that it was not only Rodrick's gun, but also the same weapon that wounded Caldwell.

The police showed that Heirens had a propensity for random acts of violence.

The potential murder weapon was also recovered, albeit in a most circuitous and unprofessional way. In his confession, Heirens claims that after he murdered and dismembered Suzanne Degnan he threw the knife he used under the tracks of the elevated subway track near the Degnan home. For some reason, the police never searched for the weapon, but when the local press learned of the details they went to the nearest subway station and asked employees if they recovered a knife in the vicinity. Workers claimed they did and handed the knife over to reporters who then gave the weapon to the police. The knife was then identified by Guy Rodrick, the man whose gun Heirens was arrested with, as having been stolen along with his gun.

The final bit of evidence that was used against Heirens was that of eye witness George Subgrunski. Subgrunski was a soldier who claimed that he saw a man loosely fitting Heirens' description walking near the Degnan residence with a bag in his hand the night of the abduction and murder. When Subgrunski was initially shown a photo lineup, he was unable to identify Heirens as the mysterious man outside the residence; but days later at a pre-trial hearing he identified Heirens while the defendant sat at his seat.

Alone, Subgrunski's testimony would not have been enough for an indictment, not even in 1946, but combined with the other evidence Heirens was looking at the death penalty.

A Plea Bargain?

As already mentioned at several points above, the landscape of the American justice system was quite different in 1946. The police had much more leeway to question and at times abuse suspects, search warrants were for the most part optional, and oftentimes suspects were considered guilty until proven innocent. The death penalty also had a ubiquitous role in American society: in the states that had the death penalty, the standard method of execution at the time, the electric chair was often referred to fondly as "old sparky."

And the appeals process did not last for several years as it does today in most states.

Today, death row inmates in some American states languish for decades before they are executed and in California death row inmates are much more likely to die of natural causes than by lethal injection, which is the standard form of execution in most states. Even in states that more routinely execute death row inmates, such as Texas, the average wait for execution is around ten years.

In 1946, death row inmates in most American states could expect to be executed within five years, which put the young William Heirens on the spot. If he decided to take his case to trial and lost, he could expect to be given the death penalty and executed before his thirtieth birthday. His other alternative was to take a plea bargain that allowed him to plead guilty to one murder and receive a life sentence that would give him a small chance of one day getting paroled.

William Tuohy, who was the prosecutor assigned to the Heirens case, offered to allow Heirens to plead guilty to one murder if he admitted to all three at a press conference on July 30, 1946. The deal would have spared Heirens from Illinois' "old sparky" by giving him *one* life sentence and a slim chance of one day seeing the outside world.

The press conference was held in Tuohy's office, where he, Heirens, Heirens' attorneys, and a gaggle of reporters assembled to hear the Lipstick Killer finally tell America why he killed those three innocent women.

The press conference turned into a fiasco.

The whole situation is another example of how much the American criminal justice system has changed in the last seventy years. Guilty pleas are almost always conducted in a courtroom, especially if the defendant is being held in custody on a charge as serious as murder, and in many states the press is not allowed to record the proceedings with cameras. In the states where the press is allowed to record the proceedings, they are not allowed to ask questions until the hearing is over and the defendant/convicted is being led away.

Tuohy delivered a monologue to the press where he outlined how the police arrested Heirens and the stack of evidence that the Cook County prosecutor's office used to obtain an indictment against him. After he was done, Tuohy answered some questions from the press and then turned the microphone over to Heirens, who was supposed to admit to all the murders following a script that he and his lawyers prepared.

The Lipstick Killer did not follow the script.

He was evasive and noncommittal with his answers, which resulted in Tuohy pulling the plea bargain and once more threatening Heirens with the death penalty.

Concerning the press conference, years later Heirens said: "It was Tuohy himself. After assembling all the officials, including attorneys and policemen, he began a preamble about how long everyone had waited to get a confession from me, but, at last, the truth was going to be told. He kept emphasizing the word 'truth' and I asked him if he really wanted the truth. He assured me that he did...Now Tuohy made a big deal about hearing the truth. Now, when I was being forced to lie to save myself. It made me angry...so I told them the truth, and everyone got very upset."

Heirens Saves His Life

Heirens' performance at the July 30 press conference put him in the cross hairs of the angry prosecutor and seemingly set him on course for Illinois' death row. Prosecutor Tuohy approached Heirens' attorneys once more with another deal, but this one was not as sweet as the first: Heirens would admit to the murders in another press conference and be sentenced to three *consecutive* life sentences, which would almost certainly mean that the young man would die in prison. Under the urging of both his attorneys and parents, Heirens decided to take the deal.

The press conference was held on August 6 in Tuohy's office and the second time proved to be more much more illuminating. Heirens recounted the details of the murders in a nineteen page confession and reenacted parts of the crimes. The written confession began: I first started to steal when I was about 10 years of age. At that early time, the mere act of stealing carried with it a certain sex satisfaction."

Tuohy then loaded Heirens and his attorneys into a Cook County Sheriff's transport vehicle and they all took a road trip to Chicago's north side to visit the three murder scenes.

They all went into the apartments where Heirens was asked specific questions about how and why he killed each of his victims. Heirens was adamant that although the burglaries themselves gave him a sexually satisfying feeling, he only killed the women and Suzanne Degnan to keep from being caught.

The highlight of the field trip was the visit to the Degnan home.

Once at the Degnan home, a throng of curious onlookers assembled outside the home to get a live look at the Lipstick Killer and perhaps see the infamous killer do or say something interesting.

For those who came to see the spectacle they were not let down.

A ladder was provided for Heirens to demonstrate how he ascended into Suzanne's bedroom where he claimed she screamed. Heirens then took a rag, put it into her mouth, and then descended the ladder with the little girl. He then brought her to the laundry room in the apartment building down the street where he killed and dismembered her.

The crowd was shocked and horrified at the account.

Heirens' detailed accounts of the crimes made some who were on the fence as to his guilt become believers in his culpability in the heinous murders. The identity of the Lipstick Killer was finally revealed.

On September 4, with his parents in attendance in the courtroom, Heirens officially pled guilty to the murders in front of Judge Harold G. Ward. The guilty plea saved Heirens from the electric chair, but that night he attempted to end his own life by hanging.

When a shift change was taking place and there were fewer guards in the cell block, Heirens took one of his bed sheets and fashioned it into a noose and tied it through the bars of his cell. He hung for several minutes before guards found him and took the unconscious Lipstick Killer down from his jailhouse noose. Heirens would later say that he tried to commit suicide out of desperation because no one believed in his innocence, but the reality is that it may have been one last attempt at control over the situation.

One thing that all serial killers have in common, no matter their background, pathology, or methodology, is the need to have control over situations. Most serial killers grow up with the feeling that they have no control over their lives, but once they begin killing they discover that the control they exert over their victims is empowering and exhilarating. The feeling they gain compels them to keep killing.

Heirens implied throughout his psychiatric interviews and in the letters to his parents that he has some of those same control issues in his life.

But once Heirens admitted in court to the three murders, he was about to lose total control over his life.

The next day Heirens was back in court where the judge formally sentenced him to three consecutive life sentences. The judge ordered the county sheriff to transfer Heirens immediately to Stateville prison in Crest Hill, Illinois.

While he was en route to the prison, Sheriff Mulcahy asked Heirens if Suzanne Degnan suffered. Heirens answered: I can't tell you if she suffered, Sheriff Mulcahy. I didn't kill her. Tell Mr. Degnan to please look after his other daughter, because whoever killed Suzanne is still out there."

The city of Chicago could breathe a bit easier knowing that the notorious burglar and serial murderer known as the Lipstick Killer was in prison for the rest of his life.

With the Lipstick Killer safely locked away in a maximum security prison, Americans quickly forgot about the horrific crimes of William Heirens. Life returned to normal in Chicago and Heirens' former classmates at the University of Chicago resumed their studies.

Even William's family seemed to move on without him.

Despite standing by his side during the criminal proceedings, shortly after Heirens pled guilty to the murders, his parents changed their family name to Hill and then divorced. Neither parent ever visited the Lipstick Killer in prison or gave interviews to the press, but it is known that his mother kept in contact with him through letters and even sent him money for some time. By the late 1980s, Heirens' father was dead and his mother was living a quiet, anonymous life in the Chicago area.

But for William, in many ways his story was just about to begin.

CHAPTER 6:
Life in Prison

Throughout history, life in American prisons has never been easy. Whether it was in the "penal farms" of the south, where inmates were forced to work long hours in the hot sun, or in the cold dreary prisons of the north, prison life in the United States was always a difficult existence. In fact, "existence" is probably the verb that best sums up how inmates, especially those confined for life sentences, live their lives behind bars, in the past and today.

Inmates are obviously deprived of the most basic freedoms and forced to live around some of the most dangerous people in the country. Life in prison alternates between long stretches of monotony and boredom interspersed from time to time with intense, extreme bouts of violence.

American prisons are also known for being notoriously dangerous places and in the 1940s, Stateville prison was one of the most violent prisons in the United States.

When Heirens entered Stateville prison in 1946 he already had two strikes against him: he was known to all the other inmates due to the high profile nature of his crime and he was a child killer.

Even some of the most hardened criminals are fathers and brothers. There is also such a thing as "honor amongst thieves" in prisons, a code, whereby an inmate-created hierarchy exists where gang leaders and career criminals are at the top, while child molesters and killers are on the bottom.

Heirens came into Stateville at the bottom of the pecking order.

At Home with His Peers

Despite the particularly heinous nature of his crimes, especially the murder of Suzanne Degnan, there is no evidence that Heirens suffered any serious assaults in prison. There is also no evidence that he assaulted any other inmates in order to keep the predators at bay. Furthermore, there is no evidence that Heirens became a prison "bitch" to make his life behind bars safer and more comfortable.

How was Heirens able to stay safe for so long in one of the United States' toughest prison systems?

The answer appears to be related to his personality. As discussed above, Heirens was a natural loner who shunned crowds of people, which behind bars can actually be an asset. Once he survived the initial shock of prison, he became just another number, literally, and so was able to navigate quietly through the often dangerous world where he lived.

Heirens also apparently made himself an asset to both prison officials and the inmate community.

As the Lipstick Killer kept his head down and away from inmate violence, he learned several vocational trades such as wood working, small engine repair, and electronics. Eventually, he took the knowledge he learned and opened his own inmate repair shop. Inmates and even guards brought Heirens their broken appliances such as radios, electric razors, and later televisions that he fixed *quid pro quo*.

The Lipstick Killer quickly became an important pillar of the prison community at Stateville as he provided a valuable service to both inmates and guards that offered him a certain level of protection. The inmates left him alone physically because he helped them with the few creature comforts they were allowed to have and the guards liked him because he was not a troublemaker.

Ultimately, Heirens was able to walk through the cellblocks and yard at Stateville safely for years primarily due to his attitude and temperament, which was actually ideally suited to a prison environment.

While Heirens did his time at Stateville, he shared the yard with some equally notorious inmates.

When the Lipstick Killer arrived in Stateville he joined another infamous Chicago child killer, Nathan Leopold. Leopold was half of the famed Leopold and Loeb duo that murdered a child in in 1924. After the two were convicted, they both eventually ended up in Stateville prison where Loeb was murdered by another inmate in 1936.

Leopold survived some close calls himself and provided somewhat of a template for Heirens by the time he arrived in Stateville in 1946. Leopold helped to reorganize the prison's library, tutored inmates, and worked in the infirmary. Although Leopold and Heirens were in the same prison during the same period, there is no evidence that the two men were friends or spent much time together; but Leopold's active life behind bars no doubt served as an inspiration for the younger Heirens.

Heirens was joined toward the end of his tenure at Stateville by another notable Chicago killer, Richard Speck. Speck was convicted of murdering eight nursing students at their home in Chicago in 1966 and sentenced to death in 1968. Speck was sent to Stateville to await his death sentence, as that was where the "death house" was at that time, but his sentence was later overturned and he was sent to general population where he lived until his death in 1991. Again, like with Leopold, it is not known how much contact Speck and Heirens had, but the former was constantly in trouble with guards and inmates and did little to contribute to the prison community, so Heirens probably avoided him.

In fact, by the time Speck strolled in to Stateville, Heirens was not only running his own repair shop, he was also working on a bachelor's of arts degree.

Today, many American prisons offer higher education opportunities to inmates, but in the 1960s it was unheard of and any inmate who wished to do so had to take the initiative. Heirens did so by enrolling in correspondence courses from over twenty different universities and earned a degree in 1972 from Lewis College, becoming the first inmate in the history of the Illinois Department of Corrections to do so.

The Lipstick Killer also used his knowledge to tutor other inmates, as Leopold did before him, and he eventually became known as a respected "jailhouse lawyer" who helped other inmates with legal matters such as appeals, lawsuits, and child custody cases.

Eventually, Heirens' good behavior and status as a respected member of the prison community earned him a transfer to the Vienna minimum security prison in Vienna, Illinois.

Towards the end of his life, as Heirens suffered from diabetes, he was transferred again to the hospital ward of the prison in Dixon, Illinois in 1998. He was by then confined to a wheelchair because of his health problems.

As Heirens counseled other inmates with their legal problems, he also worked to free himself.

Efforts to Be Released

When Heirens pled guilty to three murders in 1946, most people thought that would be the last time they heard from the Lipstick Killer. After all, he was clearly guilty and even admitted to all of the murders and several other burglaries. It was not as if a jury deliberated for several days and came to an agonizing decision to find him guilty; his own lawyers even urged him to plead guilty.

But in 1952, less than ten years into his life sentence, Heirens filed a post-conviction relief request. The crux of Heirens' argument was that the sodium pentothal injection that the authorities gave him was given without his permission and therefore a violation of his constitutional rights.

The prosecution argued that they gave the drug to Heirens not to elicit any information from him, but merely to see if he was faking a coma. The doctor who administered the drug to Heirens, Roy Grinker, reported that the Lipstick Killer showed signs of schizophrenia. Heirens argued that the report may have made a difference concerning a potential insanity defense, but its contents were never turned over to the defense or entered into the official court record.

One of the reasons that the results of the sodium pentothal treatment were not entered into the official records may have been because by the mid-1940s its use in the justice system was falling out of favor and by the 1950s it was totally discredited.

As Heirens continued to fight his convictions from behind bars, he eventually picked up some unlikely allies.

Mary Jane Blanchard, the daughter of Josephine Ross, told reporters that she supported Heirens' claims of innocence.

"I cannot believe that young Heirens murdered my mother. He just does not fit into the picture of my mother's death … I have looked at all the things Heirens stole and there was nothing of my mother's things among them," said Blanchard.

Supporters of Heirens began to pop up from coast to coast. Many of his supporters were lawyers, law students, and academics who believed that Heirens' constitutional rights to a fair trial were violated and that he therefore deserved a new trial.

There were also the serial killer groupies.

Nearly every serial killer in America over the last forty years have amassed large followings of adoring fans who write them letters and send money to their favorite killers. Serial killer trading cards, comic books, and in more recent years, websites have been created that are devoted to exploring the lives and sometimes arguing the innocence of various convicted serial killers.

William Heirens, the Lipstick Killer, was no different in this respect, although most of his support came from people who legitimately believed his rights were violated other than serial killer groupies. Both groups of Heirens supporters though coalesced to keep his case in the public eye.

Eventually, Heirens' case gained enough public attention that experts who questioned some of the forensic evidence got involved.

To begin with, there was never much forensic evidence stacked against Heirens, but the combination of handwriting analysis and fingerprints on the ransom note and on the door jamb of Frances Brown's apartment seemed rather convincing.

But over the years some came to doubt those results.

Questioning the Evidence

During the course of the initial investigation, the Chicago police called in several handwriting experts to compare Heirens' known writings with the infamous lipstick inscription on the wall of Brown's apartment and the Degnan ransom note. Herbert Walter claimed that all three shared definite similarities and so his testimony was entered into the official record, while George Schwartz claimed that they were not.

Schwartz's statements were ignored and only discovered years later by Heirens' supporters.

Both men had considerable time to view the evidence and did so on numerous occasions. At first, Walter gave a statement that Heirens was the author of the lipstick inscription or the ransom note, but weeks later he changed his opinion, which supporters of Heirens claim points to some improper activity. Walter claimed that he merely changed his opinion once he had more time to consider the evidence.

It should be pointed out that by all accounts Walter was a consummate professional and had no reason to change his testimony other than it being his true opinion. Walter worked with police departments across the United States for decades during the early and middle twentieth century with neither his methods nor integrity being called into question. In particular, Walter became a luminary in the field of handwriting analysis after he worked on the Lindbergh Kidnapping case in 1932. His testimony helped to convict Bruno Hauptman in the kidnapping and murder of Charles Lindbergh's son and he also helped solve hundreds of cases before and after the Lipstick Killer murder.

For years the opinion of Walter stood as the core of the handwriting evidence used against Heirens, but as the Lipstick Killer filed motions and briefs, other experts decided to take a look at some of the evidence.

In 1996, former FBI handwriting expert, David Grimes, argued that he believed Heirens was not the author of the note or the wall inscription; but many people thought that the opinion was done merely for the cameras and to enhance Grimes' image as he segued his career into the private and corporate world.

In the end, the handwriting evidence against Heirens may have been weak and many experts agree that if the case had went to trial and the Lipstick Killer had more competent lawyers, then the evidence may have been thrown out in court. With that said, most of those same legal experts also agreed that the inconclusive handwriting evidence was far from enough to get him exonerated.

Another piece of physical evidence that has been called into question is the alleged murder weapon of Suzanne Degnan. The hunting knife that was discovered by the subway workers was never positively determined, forensically speaking, to have been the murder weapon. Also, the recovery of the weapon by the workers and then it being given to the reporter violated the evidentiary chain of command and contaminated the evidence. But like the handwriting evidence, it was inconclusive and did nothing to prove Heirens' innocence.

Heirens and his supporters would have to search deeper to find a "smoking gun" that would free him from prison.

To the majority of people who continued to believe that Heirens was the Lipstick Killer and therefore rightfully serving a life sentence in the Illinois Department of Corrections, they pointed to the bloody finger print taken from the door jamb of Frances Brown's apartment. Fingerprints are unique and are extremely difficult to plant at a crime scene, especially with 1946 technology.

But Heirens and his supporters argued that the print may have been planted with a rolled fingerprint because it looked like one taken from an index card that the police used at that time for their records.

These allegations have been given the least attention because, as stated above, to do so with 1946 technology would have been much more difficult than stated. Yes, the police had Heirens' fingerprints on file from his previous arrests, but to "roll" the index card print onto the door jamb would have been difficult and most likely could not have been achieved on just one try, which would therefore have destroyed the print that was on file. Also, why would the police have framed Heirens for the crime? It is true that the Chicago police were under immense pressure to solve the crimes, but they had other, more attractive suspects at their disposal than a seventeen year old college student.

Of all the evidence that Heirens explained away throughout his incarceration, the door jamb fingerprint, although physically small, remained the largest obstacle to his freedom.

The weak fingerprint identification on the ransom note was also another issue raised on Heirens' behalf in the decades after the murders. Although Heirens' prints were on record with the Chicago police, the prints on the note were not matched until after his arrest. Heirens argued that this was a situation where investigators were adjusting the evidence to fit the suspect.

Once the note was discovered by police, it was given to a reporter to use in one of the several salacious stories that were printed at the time, which broke the chain of custody, similar to the alleged Degnan murder weapon, and essentially contaminated the evidence. Today, such an incident would be challenged by nearly every criminal defense attorney and would probably get the evidence thrown out of most courts. But Heirens' attorneys never challenged the note's chain of custody or the seven point finger print match, which was weak even by 1946 standards, as they essentially seemed to abdicate any type of reasonable defense of their client.

The last point in particular became a particularly salient aspect of Heirens' later legal briefs.

Under the United States Constitution, every American accused of a crime has the right to counsel, no matter the defendant's income level. If the defendant cannot afford to pay for his/her own attorney, as was the case for Heirens in 1946, then the courts appoint an attorney to the defendant at the taxpayers' expense. Attorneys are supposed to be equally zealous advocates of their clients whether they are paid a handsome sum by a rich defendant or a measly stipend by the government; but unfortunately theory does not always equate to reality.

Court appointed criminal defense attorneys are often less able and almost always underfunded and therefore unable to hire experts to counter any that the prosecutors may put in front of a judge and jury. In William Heirens's case, no experts were hired to testify on his behalf and his team of attorneys seem more interested in having their client plead guilty than they were of formulating a credible defense for a trial.

Heirens' legal team was led by brothers John, Malachy, and David Coghlan; three tough Irish-Americans who were familiar with the mean streets of Chicago and crime in general. The Coghlan brothers were used to defending local toughs: thieves, burglars, drug pushers, and other assorted crooks; but the Lipstick Killer was something totally foreign to them.

When one considers the context of the time in which the murders took place, the influence of the press on the Lipstick Killer case, and the seemingly mountain of circumstantial evidence against Heirens, then the pressure that the Coghlan brothers exerted on their client to accept the guilty plea appears more reasonable.

In a 1989 interview with Chicago criminal defense attorney and former colleague of John Coghlan, Patrick Tuite told reporters: "John was a shrewd man. Remembering the temper of the times, I don't think there's any doubt that Heirens would have died in the chair. There was probably a deal to save his life. It's similar to what Darrow did with Leopold and Loeb."

But not all attorneys shared Tuite's opinion.

Upon examination of the transcripts from the original Lipstick Killer case, it appears that the Coghlans may have went beyond merely working with the prosecutor in order to reach a plea agreement that was amicable for both sides and instead pressured Heirens into a guilty plea before he had a chance to consider all of his options.

"A lawyer has to stand against the world," said Chicago attorney Sam Adam in 1989. "John Coglan was a great attorney, and he was probably appalled, but what he did was not in the best tradition of the law. If that's what the transcript says, then Heirens didn't get proper representation."

An interesting caveat, or addendum, to the argument of ineffective counsel is that John Coglan claimed that Heirens admitted to all three murders to him, which is why he urged him to plead guilty to the crimes. There is nothing unethical about a lawyer urging a guilty client to plead guilty to a charge, it happens every day, but discussing it with others later could be viewed as a violation of the client-attorney privilege, which could be grounds for an appeal or new trial.

The judge who ruled in Heirens' 1952 post-conviction relief request did not agree as he wrote: "The court finds in particular that petitioner's counsel did not coerce him into confessing, re-enacting crimes of which he was not guilty, or into entering pleas of guilty. Furthermore, the record shows that he was warned by the court as to the consequences of his pleas and persisted in them. There is no question but that he was represented by counsel who were competent and experienced and did the very best they possibly could for him under the circumstances."

Perhaps the single greatest piece of evidence against Heirens, besides the bloody fingerprint, was his own words. Heirens made lengthy, detailed confessions to both the psychiatrists during his examination in the county jail and to the press at his public allocution. Heirens and his supporters argued that his August 6, 1946 confession in particular contained twenty nine inconsistencies with the facts of the murders.

The reality is that most of these inconsistencies were minor and in Heirens' own words to the psychiatrists, most of his crimes were like "walking through darkness" and quite "vague."

In fact, Heirens' own words years later, where he professed his innocence seemed to point towards this: "All I can say is that

I've gone over all the events and traced everything. I've searched my mind. And it's just impossible that I did it. It's not possible."

Why would an innocent man have to go through the events if he was never part of them and why would he have to search his mind for the details?

Finally, Heirens and his supporters pointed to a most intriguing suspect that they believed the Chicago police let slip through their hands.

Richard Russell Thomas

In the weeks following Heirens' murder spree in late 1945 and early 1946, the police developed a lengthy suspect list, but in the end Heirens proved to be their man. In the decades since Heirens' conviction though, he and his supporters have pointed the finger at a man who they argue was Suzanne Deganan's true killer.

During the time of the Lipstick Killer's reign of terror, Richard Russell Thomas was a forty two year old drifter from Phoenix, Arizona who occasionally worked as a nurse. At the time of the Degnan murder, Thomas was known to be in Chicago and he even confessed the crime to police, although he later recanted.

Heirens' supporters have pointed out that Thomas was previously convicted of attempted extortion for threatening to kidnap a little girl and he was a convicted burglar and child molester. More importantly, the Phoenix police noted similarities between Thomas' writing and the ransom note left at the Degnan home.

Other circumstantial evidence that pointed towards Thomas included his background in the medical field: many argued that the dismemberment of Suzanne Degnan could only have been done by someone with a medical background and with precise medical instruments.

With all of that said, the evidence against Thomas was just as circumstantial as that against Heirens and did not include a bloody fingerprint. Thomas was also never a suspect in the other two murders, namely the Lipstick Killer murder.

Ultimately, Heirens had a nearly impossible hill to climb because he pled guilty to the three murders. Nearly all people who are exonerated of guilty convictions were found guilty in a trial and therefore have the ability to stand on the argument that they never admitted to guilt. Since Heirens never had a trial in the first place it was nearly impossible for him to get one decades later without a "smoking gun" that proved his innocence and, as noted extensively above, most of the new arguments raised were inconclusive.

CHAPTER 7:
The Final Years of the Lipstick Killer

From the 1970s onward, Heirens spent his time in prison helping other inmates and working towards his own potential release.

He continued to help other inmates with their appeals, as will be discussed below in one notable case, and he volunteered at the prison's hospital infirmary. Heirens also found his artistic side and was instrumental in instituting art classes at the Vienna prison. But in the end he spent most of his free time trying to secure his own release from prison.

Not all of his efforts to be released were spent trying to prove innocence though.

Attempts at Parole and Other Legal Maneuvers

Until the 1980s, prison sentences in the United States, even for murder, were relatively light and nearly everyone sentenced to confinement at that time were later released. Parole was a viable option for most inmates before the 1980s, even convicted murderers, as long as they demonstrated that they had a reasonably good record behind bars and were genuinely contrite for their crimes.

Heirens could definitely demonstrate to any parole board that he had a good prison record and was even an asset to the prison community, but he was never contrite since that would mean he would have had to admit to the murders.

His lack of remorse was one of the major reasons he was denied parole every time he faced the board beginning in 1961 until his death in 2012.

Actually, Heirens was given institutional parole for the Degnan murder in 1965 and officially discharged from the case in 1966. After that he then had to serve the other two sentences consecutively, but by the late 1960s it looked as if Heirens may once again see the streets of Chicago.

But as Bob Dylan sang in his famous song around that time, "The times they are a changing."

After the counter-counter revolution of the 1960s and the Civil Rights movement of the 1950s and '60s, most Americans were ready to get back to basics by the 1970s. The 1970s also witnessed a dramatic spike in the crime rate throughout the United States that finally peaked in the early 1980s. All of these factors led to an increasingly conservative turn in American politics that also affected the justice system.

Gone were the days of lenient sentences and sympathetic parole boards and in their place was a get tough on crime attitude and mandatory minimum prison sentences.

But Heirens believed that he was grandfathered in under those more lenient sentencing guidelines. Under those guidelines, Heirens should have been discharged from the Brown murder in 1975, the Ross murder in 1983, and the remaining burglary charges six months later.

The Lipstick Killer saw an opportunity.

In 1983 Heirens put his knowledge to use on behalf of another inmate named Gary Welsh, who was sentenced before Illinois stiffened its sentencing guidelines and parole requirements in 1973. Heirens filed a lawsuit on behalf of Welsh that argued he could not be denied parole purely on the grounds of deterrence. The Seventh District U.S. Court of Appeals agreed, which then led to Heirens filing a parole request based on the ruling.

Heirens then filed a brief with the federal court in East Saint Louis, Illinois and found a sympathetic ear in Judge Gerald Cohn who wrote: "The uncontradicted record indicates that Heirens has long been considered by the [parole] board to be completely rehabilitated." He added that there was not, "even a shred of evidence to suggest concern on their part concerning Heirens' suitability as a parole risk."

Cohn ordered the state of Illinois to immediately release Heirens from confinement.

The state of Illinois quickly flew into an uproar.

Surviving family members of Heirens' victims, law makers, and the press all weighed in on the lack of foresight that the "bleeding heart" judge showed in his decision to release Heirens; but there was seemingly nothing they could do, unless the federal court somehow reversed its ruling.

In a controversial move that many scholars consider to have skirted the bounds of constitutionality, the Illinois Department of Corrections requested that the Seventh District Court "review" their ruling in the Welsh case.

The court gave a new ruling that essentially stated that although the old parole regulations may not have explicitly stated deterrence was one of its parameters, it was implied.

The ruling seemed to be directed directly at Heirens; meant to keep the long serving Lipstick Killer in prison for the duration of his life. Many questioned the fairness of the ruling; but academics stated that no matter how unfair it may have looked, the ruling was constitutionally sound.

It was back to the drawing board for Heirens.

The Lipstick Killer continued to apply for parole but was continually denied as he failed to show remorse for his crimes.

He filed a petition for clemency in 2002 as a last ditch effort to be released in his golden years, but that too was denied.

The Death of the Lipstick Killer

After he exhausted all potential avenues to be released, Heirens apparently became resigned with his situation and lived out his final years in the medical prison in Dixon, Illinois.

Most people hope to die around those they love and know best, usually their family members and close friends. By the time Heirens died, he had no family or loved ones on the outside: he had no children, both his parents were long dead, and he had been estranged from his only sibling for decades.

When Heirens died on March 5, 2012 he was surrounded by the people that knew him best and the people he was closet to in the world: other inmates and guards.

William Heirens spent over sixty five years in prison, which made him not only one of the longest serving inmates in the history of the Illinois Department of Corrections, but also in the United States.

Few mourned the passing of the Lipstick Killer on the outside and in fact many were relieved that the nearly seven decade saga had finally come to an end.

Betty Fin, who was the sister of Suzanne Degnan, had every reason to celebrate the killer's death and viewed his passing in a most Zen like manner.

"I hope he made amends. I never wished him ill. I just wanted him in prison for everybody's safety," she said. "It was never out of retribution. It was out of fear that he could hurt somebody else, and if we did not go to all these parole hearings and protest it and he got out and he hurt a child, you just couldn't live with it."

Conclusion

Although William Heirens, the "Lipstick Killer," is not the first person to come to mind when most think of serial killers, his case provides many interesting twists and turns that make him unique among his peers.

He does not have the kill count or prolific nature of some killers: he "only" claimed three victims and did so over a relatively short period of time in a fairly confined geographic area. He also was not known for his brutality, although any murder is brutal.

Perhaps the most interesting and important aspects of the Lipstick Killer's biography is not his actual killing spree, but the events in his life that led up to the spree and the turns that his life took later.

William Heirens grew up in a seemingly stable, loving home, which is quite different from most known serial killers. But beneath the façade of a normal, all-American teen lurked a disturbed young man who fought with a repressed sexuality and possessed strong feelings of academic and intellectual superiority over his peers. Because of those feelings, Heirens was unable to connect with other people his own age, which eventually developed into a lack of empathy for others in general.

Heirens lack of empathy led him to commit an incredible amount of burglaries and eventually three murders in the course of those crimes.

Once safely tucked away in some of America's prisons, the Lipstick Killer continued to write his story by becoming an important part of the prison community, while trying to secure his release.

It is possible that Heirens could have gone either way. After all, he showed some promise as a student and by all accounts he had a good work ethic. Maybe he would have grown out of his urges to commit burglaries or maybe he could have found help. In the end, life in the real world proved to be too much for William Heirens as he was driven to spend his nights in the shadows instead of in the light with family and friends.

Perhaps that is the defining aspect of the Lipstick Killer's life: he was never able to fit in with society on the outside and in fact proved to be a menace; but inside prison walls he found his true calling and the place where he belonged all along.

The Lipstick Killer died at home among his friends and peers.

FREE BONUS CHAPTER

The making of a serial killer

"I was born with the devil in me," said H.H. Holmes, who in 1893 took advantage of the World's Fair – and the extra room he rented out in his Chicago mansion – to kill at least 27 people without attracting much attention.

"I could not help the fact that I was a murderer, no more than the poet can help the inspiration to sing. I was born with the evil one standing as my sponsor beside the bed where I was ushered into the world, and he has been with me since," Holmes said.

The idea of "I can't help it" is one of the hallmarks of many serial killers, along with an unwillingness to accept responsibility for their actions and a refusal to acknowledge that they themselves used free will to do their dreadful deeds.

"Yes, I did it, but I'm a sick man and can't be judged by the standards of other men," said Juan Corona, who killed 25 migrant workers in California in the late 1960s and early 1970s, burying them in the very fruit orchards where they'd hoped to build a better life for their families.

Dennis Rader, who called himself the BTK Killer (Bind, Torture, Kill) also blamed some unknown facet to his personality, something he called Factor X, for his casual ability to kill one family, then go home to his own, where he was a devoted family man.

"When this monster entered my brain, I will never know, but it is here to stay. How does one cure himself? I can't stop it, the monster goes on, and hurts me as well as society. Maybe you can stop him. I can't," said Rader, who said he realized he was different than the other kids before he entered high school. "I actually think I may be possessed with demons."

But again, he blamed others for not stopping him from making his first murderous move.

"You know, at some point in time, someone should have picked something up from me and identified it," he later said.

Rader was not the only serial killer to place the blame far away from himself.

William Bonin actually took offense when a judge called him "sadistic and guilty of monstrous criminal conduct."

"I don't think he had any right to say that to me," Bonin later whined. "I couldn't help myself. It's not my fault I killed those boys."

It leaves us always asking why

For those of us who are not serial killers, the questions of why and how almost always come to mind, so ill equipped are we to understand the concept of murder on such a vast scale.

"Some nights I'd lie awake asking myself, 'Who the hell is this BTK?'" said FBI profiler John Douglas, who worked the Behavioral Science Unit at Quantico before writing several best-selling books, including "Mindhunter: Inside the FBI's Elite Serial Crime Unit," and "Obsession: The FBI's Legendary Profiler Probes the Psyches of Killers, Rapists, and Stalkers and Their Victims and Tells How to Fight Back."

The questions were never far from his mind - "What makes a guy like this do what he does? What makes him tick?" – and it's the kind of thing that keeps profilers and police up at night, worrying, wondering and waiting for answers that are not always so easily forthcoming.

Another leader into the study of madmen, the late FBI profiler Robert Ressler - who coined the terms serial killer as well as criminal profiling – also spent sleepless nights trying to piece together a portrait of many a killer, something that psychiatrist James Brussel did almost unfailingly well in 1940, when a pipe bomb killer enraged at Con Edison was terrorizing New York City.

(Brussel told police what the killer would be wearing when they arrested him, and although he was caught at home late at night, wearing his pajamas, when police asked him to dress, he emerged from his room wearing a double-breasted suit, exactly as Brussel had predicted.)

"What is this force that takes a hold of a person and pushes them over the edge?" wondered Ressler, who interviewed scores of killers over the course of his illustrious career.

In an effort to infiltrate the minds of serial killers, Douglas and Ressler embarked on a mission to interview some of the most deranged serial killers in the country, starting their journey in California, which "has always had more than its share of weird and spectacular crimes," Douglas said.

In their search for a pattern, they determined that there are essential two types of serial killers: organized and disorganized.

Organized killers

Organized killers were revealed through their crime scenes, which were neat, controlled and meticulous, with effort taken both in the crime and with their victims. Organized killers also take care to leave behind few clues once they're done.

Dean Corll was an organized serial killer. He tortured his victims overnight, carefully collecting blood and bodily fluids on a sheet of plastic before rolling them up and burying them and their possessions, most beneath the floor of a boat shed he'd rented, going there late at night under the cover of darkness.

Disorganized killers

On the flip side of the coin, disorganized killers grab their victims indiscriminately, or act on the spur of the moment, allowing victims to collect evidence beneath their fingernails when they fight back and oftentimes leaving behind numerous clues including weapons.

"The disorganized killer has no idea of, or interest in, the personalities of his victims," Ressler wrote in his book "Whoever Fights Monsters," one of several detailing his work as a criminal profiler. "He does not want to know who they are, and many times takes steps to obliterate their personalities by quickly knocking them unconscious or covering their faces or otherwise disfiguring them."

Cary Stayner – also known as the Yosemite Killer – became a disorganized killer during his last murder, which occurred on the fly when he was unable to resist a pretty park educator.

Lucky for other young women in the picturesque park, he left behind a wide range of clues, including four unmatched tire tracks from his aging 1979 International Scout.

"The crime scene is presumed to reflect the murderer's behavior and personality in much the same way as furnishings reveal the homeowner's character," Douglas and Ressler later wrote, expanding on their findings as they continued their interview sessions.

Serial killers think they're unique – but they're not

Dr. Helen Morrison – a longtime fixture in the study of serial killers who keeps clown killer John Wayne Gacy's brain in her basement (after Gacy's execution she sent the brain away for an analysis that proved it to be completely normal) – said that at their core, most serial killers are essentially the same.

While psychologists still haven't determined the motives behind what drives serial killers to murder, there are certain characteristics they have in common, said Morrison, who has studied or interviewed scores of serial killers and wrote about her experiences in "My Life Among the Serial Killers."

Most often men, serial killers tend to be talkative hypochondriacs who develop a remorseless addiction to the brutality of murder.

Too, they are able to see their victims as inanimate objects, playthings, of you will, around simply for their amusement.

Empathy? Not on your life.

"They have no appreciation for the absolute agony and terror and fear that the victim is demonstrating," said Morrison. "They just see the object in front of them. A serial murderer has no feelings. Serial killers have no motives. They kill only to kill an object."

In doing so, they satisfy their urges, and quiet the tumultuous turmoil inside of them.

"You say to yourself, 'How could anybody do this to another human being?'" Morrison said. "Then you realize they don't see them as humans. To them, it's like pulling the wings off a fly or the legs off a daddy longlegs.... You just want to see what happens. It's the most base experiment."

Nature vs. nurture?

For many serial killers, the desire to kill is as innate at their hair or eye color, and out of control, but most experts say that childhood trauma is an experience shared by them all.

In 1990, Colin Wilson and Donald Seaman conducted a study of serial killers behind bars and found that childhood problems were the most influential factors that led serial killers down their particular path of death and destruction.

Former FBI profiler Robert Ressler – who coined the terms serial killer and criminal profiling – goes so far as to say that 100 percent of all serial killers experienced childhoods that were not filled with happy memories of camping trips or fishing on the lake.

According to Ressler, of all the serial killers he interviewed or studied, each had suffered some form of abuse as a child - either sexual, physical or emotional abuse, neglect or rejection by parents or humiliation, including instances that occurred at school.

For those who are already hovering psychologically on edge due to unfortunate genetics, such events become focal points that drive a killer to act on seemingly insane instincts.

Because there is often no solid family unit – parents are missing or more focused on drugs and alcohol, sexual abuse goes unnoticed, physical abuse is commonplace – the child's development becomes stunted, and they can either develop deep-seeded rage or create for themselves a fantasy world where everything is perfect, and they are essentially the kings of their self-made castle.

That was the world of Jeffrey Dahmer, who recognized his need for control much later, after hours spent in analysis where he learned the impact of a sexual assault as a child as well as his parents' messy, rage-filled divorce.

"After I left the home, that's when I started wanting to create my own little world, where I was the one who had complete control," Dahmer said. "I just took it way too far."

Dahmer's experiences suggest that psychopathic behavior likely develops in childhood, when due to neglect and abuse, children revert to a place of fantasy, a world where the victimization of the child shifts toward others.

"The child becomes sociopathic because the normal development of the concepts of right and wrong and empathy towards others is retarded because the child's emotional and social development occurs within his self-centered fantasies. A person can do no wrong in his own world and the pain of others is of no consequence when the purpose of the fantasy world is to satisfy the needs of one person," according to one expert.

As the lines between fantasy and reality become blurred, fantasies that on their own are harmless become real, and monsters like Dean Corll find themselves strapping young boys down to a wooden board, raping them, torturing them and listening to them scream, treating the act like little more than a dissociative art project that ends in murder.

Going inside the mind:
Psychopathy and other mental illnesses

While not all psychopaths are serial killers – many compulsive killers do feel some sense of remorse, such as Green River Killer Gary Ridgeway did when he cried in court after one victim's father offered Ridgeway his forgiveness – those who are, Morrison said, are unable to feel a speck of empathy for their victims.

Their focus is entirely on themselves and the power they are able to assert over others, especially so in the case of a psychopath.

Psychopaths are charming — think Ted Bundy, who had no trouble luring young women into his car by eliciting sympathy with a faked injury — and have the skills to easily manipulate their victims, or in some cases, their accomplices.

Dean Corll was called a Svengali — a name taken from a fictional character in George du Maurier's 1895 novel "Trilby" who seduces, dominates and exploits the main character, a young girl — for being able to enlist the help of several neighborhood boys who procured his youthful male victims without remorse, even when the teens were their friends.

Some specific traits of serial killers, determined through years of profiling, include:

- **Smooth talking but insincere.** Ted Bundy was a charmer, the kind of guy that made it easy for people to be swept into his web. "I liked him immediately, but people like Ted can fool you completely," said Ann Rule, author of the best-selling "Stranger Beside Me," about her experiences with Bundy, a man she considered a friend. "I'd been a cop, had all that psychology — but his mask was perfect. I say that long acquaintance can help you know someone. But you can never be really sure. Scary."

- **Egocentric and grandiose.** Jack the Ripper thought the world of himself, and felt he would outsmart police, so much so that he sent letters taunting the London officers. "Dear Boss," he wrote, "I keep on hearing the police have caught me but they won't fix me just yet. I have laughed when they look so clever and talk about being on the right track. That joke about Leather Apron gave me real fits. I am down on whores and I shan't quit ripping them till I do get buckled. Grand work the last job was. I gave the lady no time to squeal. How can they catch me now? I love my work and want to start again. You will soon hear of me with my funny little games. I saved some of the proper red stuff in a ginger beer bottle over the last job to write with but it went thick like glue and I can't use it. Red ink is fit enough I hope ha. ha. The next job I do I shall clip the lady's ears off and send to the police officers … My knife's so nice and sharp I want to get to work right away if I get a chance. Good luck."

- **Lack of remorse or guilt.** Joel Rifkin was filled with self-pity after he was convicted of killing and dismembering at least nine women. He called his conviction a tragedy, but later, in prison, he got into an argument with mass murderer Colin Ferguson over whose killing spree was more important, and when Ferguson taunted him for only killing women, Rifkin said, "Yeah, but I had more victims."

- **Lack of empathy.** Andrei Chikatilo, who feasted on bits of genitalia both male and female after his kills, thought nothing of taking a life, no matter how torturous it was for his victims. "The whole thing - the cries, the blood, the agony - gave me relaxation and a certain pleasure," he said.

- **Deceitful and manipulative.** John Wayne Gacy refused to take responsibility for the 28 boys buried beneath his house, even though he also once said that clowns can get away with murder. "I think after 14 years under truth serum had I committed the crime I would have known it," said the man the neighbors all claimed to like. "There's got to be something that would... would click in my mind. I've had photos of 21 of the victims and I've looked at them all over the years here and I've never recognized anyone of them."

- **Shallow emotions.** German serial killer Rudolph Pliel, convicted of killing 10 people and later took his own life in prison, compared his "hobby" of murder to playing cards, and later told police, "What I did is not such a great harm, with all these surplus women nowadays. Anyway, I had a good time."

- **Impulsive.** Tommy Lynn Sells, who claimed responsibility for dozens of murders throughout the Midwest and South, saw a woman at a convenience store and followed her home, an impulse he was unable to control. He waited until the house went dark, then "I went into this house. I go to the first bedroom I see...I don't know whose room it is and, and, and, and I start stabbing." The victim was the woman's young son.

- **Poor behavior controls.** "I wished I could stop but I could not. I had no other thrill or happiness," said UK killer Dennis Nilsen, who killed at least 12 young men via strangulation, then bathed and dressed their bodies before disposing of them, often by burning them.
- **Need for excitement.** For Albert Fish - a masochistic killer with a side of sadism that included sending a letter to the mother of one of his victims, describing in detail how he cut, cooked and ate her daughter - even the idea of his own death was one he found particularly thrilling. "Going to the electric chair will be the supreme thrill of my life," he said.
- **Lack of responsibility.** "I see myself more as a victim rather than a perpetrator," said Gacy, in a rare moment of admitting the murders. "I was cheated out of my childhood. I should never have been convicted of anything more serious than running a cemetery without a license. They were just a bunch of worthless little queers and punks."
- **Early behavior problems.** "When I was a boy I never had a friend in the world," said German serial killer Heinrich Pommerencke, who began raping and murdering girls as a teen.

- **Adult antisocial behavior.** Gary Ridgeway pleaded guilty to killing 48 women, mostly prostitutes, who were easy prey and were rarely reported missing – at least not immediately. "I don't believe in man, God nor Devil. I hate the whole damned human race, including myself... I preyed upon the weak, the harmless and the unsuspecting. This lesson I was taught by others: Might makes right."

'I felt like it'

Many psychopaths will say after a crime, "I did it because I felt like it," with a certain element of pride.

That's how BTK killer Dennis Rader felt, and because he had no sense of wrong regarding his actions, he was able to carry on with his normal life with his wife and children with ease.

Someone else's demeanor might have changed, they may have become jittery or anxious, and they would have been caught.

Many serial killers are so cold they are can pop into a diner right after a murder, never showing a sign of what they've done.

"Serial murderers often seem normal," according to the FBI. "They have families and/or a steady job."

"They're so completely ordinary," Morrison added. "That's what gets a lot of victims in trouble."

That normalcy is often what allows perpetrators to get away with their crimes for so long.

Unlike mass murderers such as terrorists who generally drop off the radar before perpetrating their event, serial killers blend in. They might seem a bit strange – neighbors noticed that Ed Gein wasn't too big on personal hygiene, and neighbors did think it was odd that William Bonin hung out with such young boys - but not so much so that anyone would ask too many questions.

"That's why so many people often say, "I had no idea" or "He was such a nice guy" after a friend or neighbor is arrested.

And it's also why people are so very, very stunned when they see stories of serial killers dominating the news.

"For a person with a conscience, Rader's crimes seem hideous, but from his point of view, these are his greatest accomplishments and he is anxious to share all of the wonderful things he has done," said Jack Levin, PhD, director of the Brudnick Center on Violence and Conflict at Northeastern University in Boston and the author of "Extreme Killings."

A new take on psychopathy

Psychopathy is now diagnosed as antisocial personality disorder, a prettier spin on an absolutely horrifying diagnosis.

According to studies, almost 50 percent of men in prison and 21 percent of women in prison have been diagnosed with antisocial personality disorder.

Of serial killers, Ted Bundy (who enjoyed sex with his dead victims), John Wayne Gacy and Charles Manson (who encouraged others to do his dirty work which included the murder of pregnant Sharon Tate) were all diagnosed with this particular affliction, which allowed them to carry out their crimes with total disregard toward others or toward the law.

They showed no remorse.

Schizophrenia

Many known serial killers were later diagnosed with some other form of mental illness, including schizophrenia, believed to be behind the crimes of David Berkowitz (he said his neighbor's dog told him to kill his six victims in the 1970s), Ed Gein, whose grisly saving of skin, bones and various female sex parts was a desperate effort to resurrect his death mother and Richard Chase (the vampire of Sacramento, who killed six people in California in order to drink their blood).

Schizophrenia includes a wide range of symptoms, ranging from hallucinations and delusions to living in a catatonic state.

Borderline personality disorder

Borderline personality disorder – which is characterized by intense mood swings, problems with interpersonal relationships and impulsive behaviors – is also common in serial killers.

Some diagnosed cases of borderline personality disorder include Aileen Wuornos, a woman whose horrific childhood and numerous sexual assaults led her to murder one of her rapists, after which she spiraled out of control and killed six other men who picked her up along with highway in Florida, nurse Kristen H. Gilbert, who killed four patients at a Virginia hospital with overdoses of epinephrine, and Dahmer, whose murder count rose to 17 before he was caught.

With a stigma still quite present regarding mental illness, it's likely we will continue to diagnose serial killers and mass murderers after the fact, too late to protect their victims.

Top signs of a serial killer

While there is still no simple thread of similarities – which is why police and the FBI have more trouble in real life solving crimes than they do on shows like "Criminal Minds" – there are some things to look for, experts say.

- **Antisocial Behavior.** Psychopaths tend to be loners, so if a child that was once gregarious and outgoing becomes shy and antisocial, this could be an issue.

Jeffrey Dahmer was a social, lively child until his parents moved to Ohio for his father's new job. There, he regressed – allegedly after being sexually molested – and began focusing his attentions on dissecting road kill rather than developing friendships.

- **Arson.** Fire is power, and power and control are part of the appeal for serial killers, who enjoy having their victims at their mercy. David Berkowitz was a pyromaniac as a child – his classmates called him Pyro as a nickname, so well-known was he for his fire obsession - and he reportedly started more than 1,000 fires in New York before he became the Son of Sam killer.

- **Torturing animals.** Serial killers often start young, and test boundaries with animals including family or neighborhood pets. According to studies, 70 percent of violent offenders have episodes of animal abuse in their childhood histories, compared to just 6 percent of nonviolent offenders. Albert DeSalvo – better known as the Boston Strangler – would capture cats and dogs as a child and trap them in boxes, shooting arrows at the defenseless animals for sport.

- **A troubled family history.** Many serial killers come from families with criminal or psychiatric histories or alcoholism. Edmund Kemper killed his grandparents to see what it would be like, and later – after he murdered a string of college students – he killed his alcoholic mother, grinding her vocal chords in the garbage disposal in an attempt to erase the sound of her voice.

- **Childhood abuse.** William Bonin – who killed at least 21 boys and young men in violent rapes and murders – was abandoned as a child, sent to live in a group home where he himself was sexually assaulted. The connections suggest either a rage that can't be erased – Aileen Wuornos, a rare female serial killer, was physically and sexually abused throughout her childhood, resulting in distrust of others and a pent-up rage that exploded during a later rape - or a disassociation of sorts, refusing to connect on a human level with others for fear of being rejected yet again.
- **Substance abuse.** Many serial killers use drugs or alcohol. Jeffrey Dahmer was discharged from the Army due to a drinking problem he developed in high school, and he used alcohol to lure his victims to his apartment, where he killed them in a fruitless effort to create a zombie-like sex slave who would never leave him.
- **Voyeurism.** When Ted Bundy was a teen, he spent his nights as a Peeping Tom, hoping to get a glimpse of one of the neighborhood girls getting undressed in their bedrooms.

- **Serial killers are usually smart.** While their IQ is not usually the reason why serial killers elude police for so long, many have very high IQs. Edmund Kemper was thisclose to being considered a genius (his IQ was 136, just four points beneath the 140 mark that earns genius status), and he used his intelligence to create complex cons that got him released from prison early after killing his grandparents, allowing eight more women to die.
- **Can't keep a job.** Serial killers often have trouble staying employed, either because their off-hours activities take up a lot of time (Jeffrey Dahmer hid bodies in his shower, the shower he used every morning before work, because he was killing at such a fast rate) or because their obsessions have them hunting for victims when they should be on the clock.

Trademarks of a serial killer

While what we know helps us get a better understanding of potential serial killers – and perhaps take a closer look at our weird little neighbors – it is still tricky for police and FBI agents to track serial killers down without knowing a few tells.

The signature

While serial killers like to stake a claim over their killings – "Serial killers typically have some sort of a signature," according to Dr. Scott Bonn, a professor at Drew University in New Jersey – they are usually still quite neat, and a signature does not necessarily mean evidence.

"Jack the Ripper, of course, his signature was the ripping of the bodies," said Bonn.

While there are multiple theories, Jack the Ripper has yet to be identified, despite the similarities in his murders.

Too, the Happy Face Killer, Keith Hunter Jespersen – whose childhood was marked by alcoholic parents, teasing at school and a propensity to abuse small animals - drew happy faces on the numerous letters he sent to both media and authorities, teasing them a bit with a carrot on a string.

"If the forensic evidence itself - depending upon the bones or flesh or whatever is left - if it allows for that sort of identification, that would be one way of using forensic evidence to link these murders," Bonn said.

The cooling off period

Organized killers are so neat, tidy and meticulous that they may never leave clues, even if they have a signature.

And if there's a long cooling off period between crimes, tracking the killer becomes even more of a challenge.

After a murder – which could be compared to a sexual experience or getting high on drugs – the uncontrollable urges that led the killer to act dissipate, at least temporarily.

But according to Ressler, serial killers are rarely satisfied with their kills, and each one increases desire – in the same way a porn addiction can start with the pages of Playboy then turn into BDSM videos or other fetishes when Playboy pictorials are no longer satisfying.

"I was literally singing to myself on my way home, after the killing. The tension, the desire to kill a woman had built up in such explosive proportions that when I finally pulled the trigger, all the pressures, all the tensions, all the hatred, had just vanished, dissipated, but only for a short time," said David Berkowitz, better known as the Son of Sam.

Afterwards, the memory of the murder, or mementos from the murder such as the skulls Jeffrey Dahmer retained, the scalps collected by David Gore or the box of vulvas Ed Gein kept in his kitchen, no longer become enough, and the killers must kill again, creating a "serial" cycle.

That window between crimes usually becomes smaller, however, which allows authorities to notice similarities in murder scenes or methodology, making tracking easier.

In the case of William Bonin, there were months between his first few murders, but toward the end, he sometimes killed two young men a day to satisfy his increasingly uncontrollable urges.

"Sometimes... I'd get tense and think I was gonna go crazy if I couldn't get some release, like my head would explode. So I'd go out hunting. Killing helped me... It was like ... needing to go gambling or getting drunk. I had to do it," Bonin said.

Hunting in pairs

Some serial killers – between 10 and 25 percent - find working as a team more efficient, and they use their charm as the hook to lure in accomplices.

Ed Gein may never have killed anyone had his accomplice, a mentally challenged man who helped Gein dig up the graves of women who resembled his mother, not been sent to a nursing home, leaving Gein unable to dig up the dead on his own.

Texas killer Dean Corll used beer, drugs, money and candy to bribe neighborhood boys to bring him their friends for what they were promised was a party, but instead would turn to torture and murder. He would have killed many more if one of his accomplices had not finally shot him to prevent another night of death.

William Bonin also liked to work with friends, and he enticed boys who were reportedly on the low end of the IQ scale to help him sadistically rape and torture his victims.

Other red flags

According to the FBI's Behavioral Science Unit – founded by Robert Ressler - 60 percent of murderers whose crimes involved sex were childhood bed wetters, and sometimes carried the habit into adulthood. One such serial killer, Alton Coleman, regularly wet his pants, earning the humiliating nickname "Pissy."

Sexual arousal over violent fantasies during puberty can also play a role in a serial killer's future.

Jeffrey Dahmer hit puberty about the same time he was dissecting road kill, so in some way, his wires became crossed and twisted, and sex and death aroused him.

Brain damage? Maybe

While Helen Morrison's test found that John Wayne Gacy's brain was normal, and Jeffrey Dahmer's father never had the opportunity to have his son's brain studied, although both he and Jeffrey had wanted the study, there is some evidence that some serial killers have brain damage that impact their ability to exact rational control.

"Normal parents? Normal brains? I think not," said Dr. Jonathan Pincus, a neurologist and author of the book "Base Instincts: What Makes Killers Kill."

"Abusive experiences, mental illnesses and neurological deficits interplayed to produce the tragedies reported in the newspapers. The most vicious criminals have also been, overwhelmingly, people who have been grotesquely abused as children and have paranoid patterns of thinking," said Pincus in his book, adding that childhood traumas can impact the developmental anatomy and functioning of the brain.

***

So what do we know?

Serial killers can be either uber-smart or brain damaged, completely people savvy or totally awkward, high functioning and seemingly normal or unable to hold down a job.

But essentially, no matter what their back story, their modus operandi or their style, "they're evil," said criminal profiler Pat Brown.

And do we need to know anything more than that?

More books by Jack Rosewood

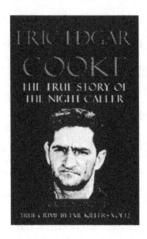

The Night Caller, The Nedlands Monster, and Eric Edgar Cooke, are the names used to describe one of the most brutal serial killers in Australian History. Over the space of 5 years, he not only murdered 8 people, he also attempted to murder 14 others, because he just wanted to hurt people. Was he crazy?

Nobody was safe from Eric Edgar Cooke. He was an opportunistic killer, selecting victims randomly. Whoever crossed his path during those hot humid nights would fall victim to his variety of killing methods. You were not safe in your homes, or walking down the road at night.

This serial killer biography will delve into the life and eventual execution of Eric Edgar Cooke, the last man hanged for murder in Perth, Western Australia. The deeds of Eric Edgar Cooke created fear and horror in the people of Perth. The true accounts from the survivors will show you how they lived through this Australian true crime.

If you are a lover of serial killers true crime, you will be enthralled by this investigative book. You will discover how it is that he could get away with his crimes for so long. Why is it that the detectives thought he was just a likeable rogue and petty thief? Discover how one man could change the lives of an entire town and become a bogeyman character for decades after his death. True crime murder doesn't get more complexing or bewildering as the story of Eric Edgar Cooke.

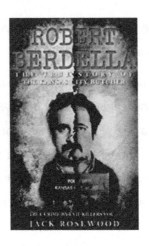

When Chris Bryson was discovered nude and severely beaten stumbling down Charlotte Street in Kansas City in 1988, Police had no idea they were about to discover the den of one of the most sadistic American serial killers in recent history. This is the true historical story of Robert Berdella, nicknamed by the media the Kansas City Butcher, who from between 1984 and 1988 brutally raped, tortured and ultimately dismembered 6 young male prostitutes in his unassuming home on a quiet street in Kansas City.

Based on the actual 720 page detailed confession provided by Berdella to investigators, it represents one of the most gruesome true crime stories of all time and is unique in the fact that it details each grizzly murder as told by the killer himself. From how he captured each man, to the terrifying methods he used in his torture chamber, to ultimately how he disposed of their corpses - rarely has there ever been a case where a convicted serial killer confessed to police in his own words his crimes in such disturbing detail.

Horrific, shocking and rarely equaled in the realms of sadistic torture – Berdella was a sexually driven lust killer and one of the most sadistic sex criminals ever captured. Not for the faint of heart, this is the tale of Robert "Bob" Berdella, the worst serial killer in Kansas City History and for those that are fans of historical serial killers, is a true must read.

Richmond, Virginia: On the morning of October 19, 1979, parolee James Briley stood before a judge and vowed to quit the criminal life. That same day, James met with brothers Linwood, Anthony, and 16-year-old neighbor Duncan Meekins. What they planned—and carried out—would make them American serial-killer legends, and reveal to police investigators a 7-month rampage of rape, robbery, and murder exceeding in brutality already documented cases of psychopaths, sociopaths, and sex criminals.

As reported in this book, the Briley gang were responsible for the killing of 11 people (among these, a 5-year-old boy and his pregnant mother), but possibly as many as 20. Unlike most criminals, however, the Briley gang's break-ins and robberies were purely incidental—mere excuses for rape and vicious thrill-kills. When authorities (aided by plea-bargaining Duncan Meekins) discovered the whole truth, even their tough skins crawled. Nothing in Virginian history approached the depravities, many of which were committed within miles of the Briley home, where single father James Sr. padlocked himself into his bedroom every night.

But this true crime story did not end with the arrests and murder convictions of the Briley gang. Linwood, younger brother James, and 6 other Mecklenburg death-row inmates, hatched an incredible plan of trickery and manipulation—and escaped from the "state-of-the-art" facility on May 31, 1984. The biggest death-row break-out in American history.

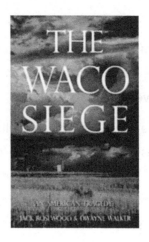

During fifty one days in early 1993 one of the most tragic events in American crime history unfolded on the plains outside Waco, Texas. An obscure and heavily armed religious sect called the Branch Davidians was barricaded inside their commune and outside were hundreds of law enforcement angry because the former had killed four ATF agents in a botched raid. Open the pages of this book and go on an engaging and captivating ride to examine one of the most important true crime stories in recent decades. Read the shocking true story of how a man the government considered a psychopath, but whose followers believed to be a prophet, led a breakaway sect of the Seventh Day Adventist Church into infamy.

You will follow the meteoric rise of the Branch Davidians' charismatic leader, David Koresh, as he went from an awkward kid in remedial classes to one of the most infamous cult leaders in world history. But the story of the Waco Siege begins long before the events of 1993. At the core of the conflict between the Branch Davidians and the United States government were ideas and interpretations of religious freedom and gun ownership, which as will be revealed in the pages of this book, a considerable philosophical gulf existed between the two sides. David Koresh and the Branch Davidians carried on a long tradition in American and Texas history of religious dissent, but in 1993 that dissent turned tragically violent.

You will find that beyond the standard media portrayals of the Waco Siege was an event comprised of complex human characters on both sides of the firing line and that perhaps the most tragic aspect of the event was that the extreme bloodshed could have been avoided.

The pages of this book will make you angry, sad, and bewildered; but no matter the emotions evoke, you will be truly moved by the events of the Waco Siege.

When Killing Cousins David Alan Gore and Fred Waterfield realized as teens that they shared the same sick, twisted sex fantasies of raping helpless, bound women who were completely at their mercy, Florida's quiet Vero Beach would be never be the same.

Some of the least remorseful of all American serial killers, the deadly duo stalked their victims, often hitchhikes they believed would never be missed, using Gore's auxiliary deputy badge as a ruse to lure them into their vehicle. After that, they were most likely to be driven to their deaths.

Their evil, sadistic story from the annals of Florida history is one that will chill even longtime fans of true crime murder, especially after reading excerpts from the letters Gore wrote from prison, in which he shared deplorable secrets that made him one of the most demented sex criminals of all time.

Gore once told a psychologist that "the devil made me do it," but those who came in contact with Gore – including the law enforcement officials that ultimately put him on Death Row – believed he was the devil due to his depraved levels of cruelty.

Among the psychopaths and sociopaths that have walked the earth, Gore was one of the worst, although those who knew them say that it was Fred Waterfield, the more popular cousin who always played the good guy to Gore's bad, who was the true brains of the outfit. As it happens, he probably was, because Waterfield almost got away with murder.

GET THE BOOK ABOUT HERBERT MULLIN FOR FREE

**Go to www.jackrosewood.com
and get this E-Book for free!**

A Note From The Author

Hello, this is Jack Rosewood. Thank you for reading this book. I hope you enjoyed the read of this chilling story. If you did, I'd appreciate if you would take a few moments to post a review on Amazon.

I would also love if you'd sign up to my newsletter to receive updates on new releases, promotions and a FREE copy of my Herbert Mullin E-Book at <u>www.jackrosewood.com</u>

Thanks again for reading this book, make sure to follow me on Facebook at Jack Rosewood Author.

A big thanks to Dwayne Walker who co-wrote this book with me.

Best Regards
Jack Rosewood

Made in the USA
Monee, IL
25 April 2024

57520819R00079